HEARTWOOD

HEARTWOOD

A LIMITED FIRST EDITION

Rick Steber   Bonanza Publishing   Don Gray

HEARTWOOD

Volume 1
HEART OF THE WEST SERIES

Writing and Photography
by
Rick Steber

Illustrations
by
Don Gray

BONANZA PUBLISHING . BOX 204 . PRINEVILLE, OREGON

Credits

Writing — Rick Steber

Photography & design — Rick Steber

Illustrations — Don Gray

Editing & typesetting — Kristi Steber

Graphic designs — Marty Todd

Color separations and Scanart halftones by Wy'east Color, Inc., Portland, Oregon — Steven Fazzolari

Text paper, 80# Frostbrite Matte, End Sheets, Astroparch Ancient Gold — Supplied by West Coast Paper Company, Portland, Oregon

Foil stamping — Golden Pacific Embossing, Seattle, Washington

Printing by Maverick Publications, Inc., Bend, Oregon — Gary Asher, Tom Healy, Ron Wells, Rebecca Chambers, Bernice Rhodes, Bridget Wise and Susan Faerber

Hardbinding by Oregon Bookbinding Company, Silverton, Oregon — Steve Kaufman

Bonanza Publishing
Box 204
Prineville, Oregon 97754

Library of Congress Catalog Card Number 91-76429

ISBN 0-945134-26-6 Hardbound Edition
ISBN 0-945134-27-4 Perfectbound Edition

"*Happy is the man to whom every tree is a friend.*"

John Muir

HEART OF THE WEST SERIES

FORWARD

Alone on the western landscape. Come, be absorbed into the open spaces where horizons are hinged by the ragged blue of mountain ranges. Look closely. See the free-roaming mustang leaving a thin trail of dust to mark its passing. See the footprint of a mountain lion pressed into black volcanic soil, a golden eagle spinning slow circles on a rising thermal, salmon surging upstream in quicksilver flashes, sunsets and rainbows painted with the same vivid palette. Let your ears ring with stillness. Feel the grit of the sand, the feathery touch of a wayward breeze. Taste the bite of the air....

The people of the West are sculpted from this land, these people who measure their existence by seasons, by cycles, by generations. Some find strength in the land, are nourished by it; others fight it as if it were their adversary. But all in all they stay because they have a love in their hearts for this place we call the West.

The West I know is woven from the fabric of the land and stitched with the lives of the people. Such a rich tapestry of memories; invited to join Nez Perce elders in their sweat lodge, sleeping in the same line shack, the very bed, where Pete French was laid to rest after being shot by a homesteader, hearing the anguish in the voice of the old rancher telling that his children have all moved away, taken jobs in the city, and now he is having to sell off the home place. But he cannot sell it all at once. So he sells one cow at a time, one bull at a time, one horse at a time. And when the stock is gone, he says, "Then, maybe, I can sell the land."

I give thanks for having the opportunity to rub shoulders with the folks who came West, who settled on raw land and carved a productive and useful life for themselves, their families and the generations who will follow. They are a dying breed, alone and forgotten, being swept away by passing time and a shrinking world.

INTRODUCTION

A tree holds its youth to its heart, developing in concentric circles from the inside out. Each circle represents a season of growth, followed by a period of dormancy.

The heartwood of a tree is a darker color than the sapwood because it has tasted the soil longer. As each ring of life is added the inner rings compress, giving the tree a backbone of supple strength which allows it to bend in the wind and bow to heavy snow without breaking.

Like the growth of a tree, the history of the West has occurred in cycles, eras, rings of expansion and evolution. One generation pushed westward for furs, the next for gold, followed by land-hungry pioneers, timber-hungry loggers.... They built layer upon layer. To plot our future course the emerging West must never lose sight of the past, and of the people who are our heartwood.

DOUGLAS FIR

CHAPTER 1

Douglas fir is common throughout the West but the best stands grow in the fertile soil and moist, mild climate west of the Sierra Nevada and Cascade mountain ranges. The trees are fast-growing and second in size only to the giant California sequoias. They are durable and live for more than a thousand years.

It takes a special breed of men to harvest the monarchs of the woods. It is dangerous work and Harold Morgan knows about that danger. Seated in a nursing home wheelchair he tells of his accident, one small mistake that forever changed the path of his life.

Ida Dutcher was a transplant. She came to the high desert in a covered wagon but never felt at peace with the land until she and her husband settled in the deep, lush woods of the coast range. Here they took root.

More than fifty years ago, on the treeless plains of southern Idaho, Ethyl Parish planted a fir seedling in her front yard. She packed water to it in a bucket and nurtured it. And then one hot summer day, in the shade of that tree, her world began to unravel.

Bridge Maley and Babe McVay spent their lives harvesting the virgin forests of Douglas fir and without a doubt some of the hardiness, the resilience of the tree, rubbed off on them.

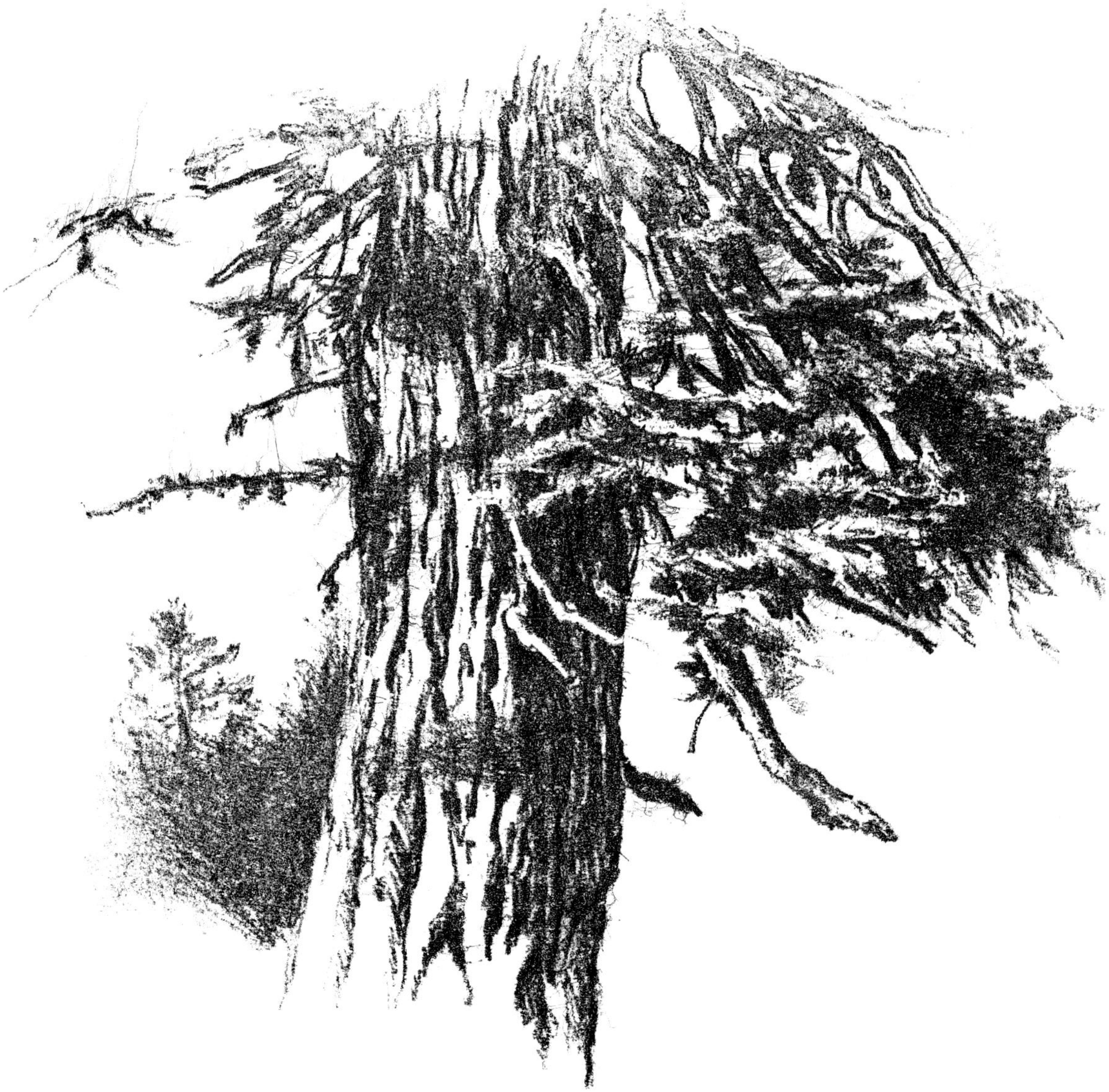

HAROLD MORGAN

Harold Morgan shifts his weight in the nursing home wheelchair, tucks a lap blanket around his legs and talks about better times.

"I went to work in the woods back in the days of horse logging. After Pearl Harbor was bombed I switched to high-lead. But the spice of my life was high climbing; topping and rigging trees.

"A high climber could do no wrong. He was the glamour boy of the woods. Never will forget being up there on top — had nerves of steel — looking out over the country, breeze in my face, quiet as the dead of night....

"Highest tree I ever topped was 210 feet. Height doesn't matter because anything over 50 feet will kill you sure as heck. After I topped the big one the tree swung back and forth and I almost could touch the seat of my pants on either side of the canyon wall."

Harold talks reverently about his days as a logger. He stops, clears his throat, continues. "It all ended July 6, 1944, the day before my 29th birthday. That was the day of my accident.

"We were working a high lead outfit and the cable should have been on a guy and shackle where it would play over our heads but it came off, caught me, knocked me into a stump and broke my neck. Was out like a light. Guess the boys packed me to the landing, put me in the back of a pickup, brought me out of the woods.

"I came to in the hospital. Tried to talk. All I could do was whisper. Told one of the boys, 'Take off my boots. I don't wanna die with my caulks on.'

"'Am I gonna make it?' I wanted to know and was told, 'Hell yes, you'll make it.' Would have felt relieved if I hadn't been paralyzed from my neck down. Once the shock wore off the hurting began. Oh my God, did I hurt!

"My brothers, they were loggers, too, came in and stayed with me. They thought I was asleep. I heard one of them crying and he said, 'Poor little guy'll never live to see morning light.' But I toughed it out. Finally, on about the third day, I moved my thumb on my right hand, wiggled it back and forth a couple of times, and then and there I knew I was going to make it.

"Ahead of me were some frightful times. Got hooked on morphine. Dreamed I was being chased by stumps and flailing roots. They dried me out, sent me home. I was depressed, crazy depressed. In such a bad way I put a gun to my head, flipped off the safety before it dawned on me what I was doing.

Scared me so bad I sold the gun.

"And then to top it all, the wife she says she can't cope with the situation. She left me with the two children — a boy, six, and a girl, four. The night she pulled out she told me, 'The only reason I married you was to get away from home. I never did love you.' Told her, 'Thanks a lot, honey.'

"Having the kids probably saved me. The responsibility. I got a job at the Wolf Point lookout, on the summit of the coast range. Took the kids with me. They were more or less raised on lookouts. Was with the Forest Service for 23 seasons.

"My recreation was, and still is, my writing. Do it long hand on a yellow, legal-size pad. When I write my imagination runs wild. The first book I did was *Caulked Boots*. It more or less tells my life's story. In there I have about logging, lots of personal stuff, too, like the time when I was a kid and the coyotes got into the sheep and about the old sow I bought for ten bucks and she was supposed to be bred but I never got a single pig out of her and then she up and died and I wasn't even able to sell her for soap grease.

"The second book, *Losers*, is about logging and World War II. It's a story I thought up. The third book, *The Wasted Years*, is a novel. I paid for the books to be published out of my own pocket. Don't figure to ever make a dime. That's not why I write. I write to lose myself in the words. Write, and there is no pain, no headaches, no hurting. Makes me even forget I'm in a nursing home. Write, and I can be young and strong. Throw up the rope. Climb. Throw up the rope. Climb...."

IDA DUTCHER

On the way to the old Dutcher place the narrow highway twists, humps and doubles back on itself as it precariously clings to the canyon wall above the rapid-choked Siuslaw River. A canopy of towering fir trees and moss-laden boughs blocks out the gray, drippy sky. Delicate ferns, bursts of pinkish-purple foxglove and tangles of blackberry brush crowd close to the oil road.

A doe and a pair of spotted fawns stand unmoving at the apron of a large meadow. At the far end of the opening the forest resumes and ancient firs stand like sentinels over several homes. Out in the open children play a game of baseball. A lazy dog struggles to its feet, stands, barking a warning.

Ida Dutcher throws open the door and maneuvers her wheelchair onto the porch, waves and hollers, "Ignore the dog and the kids. Come on in."

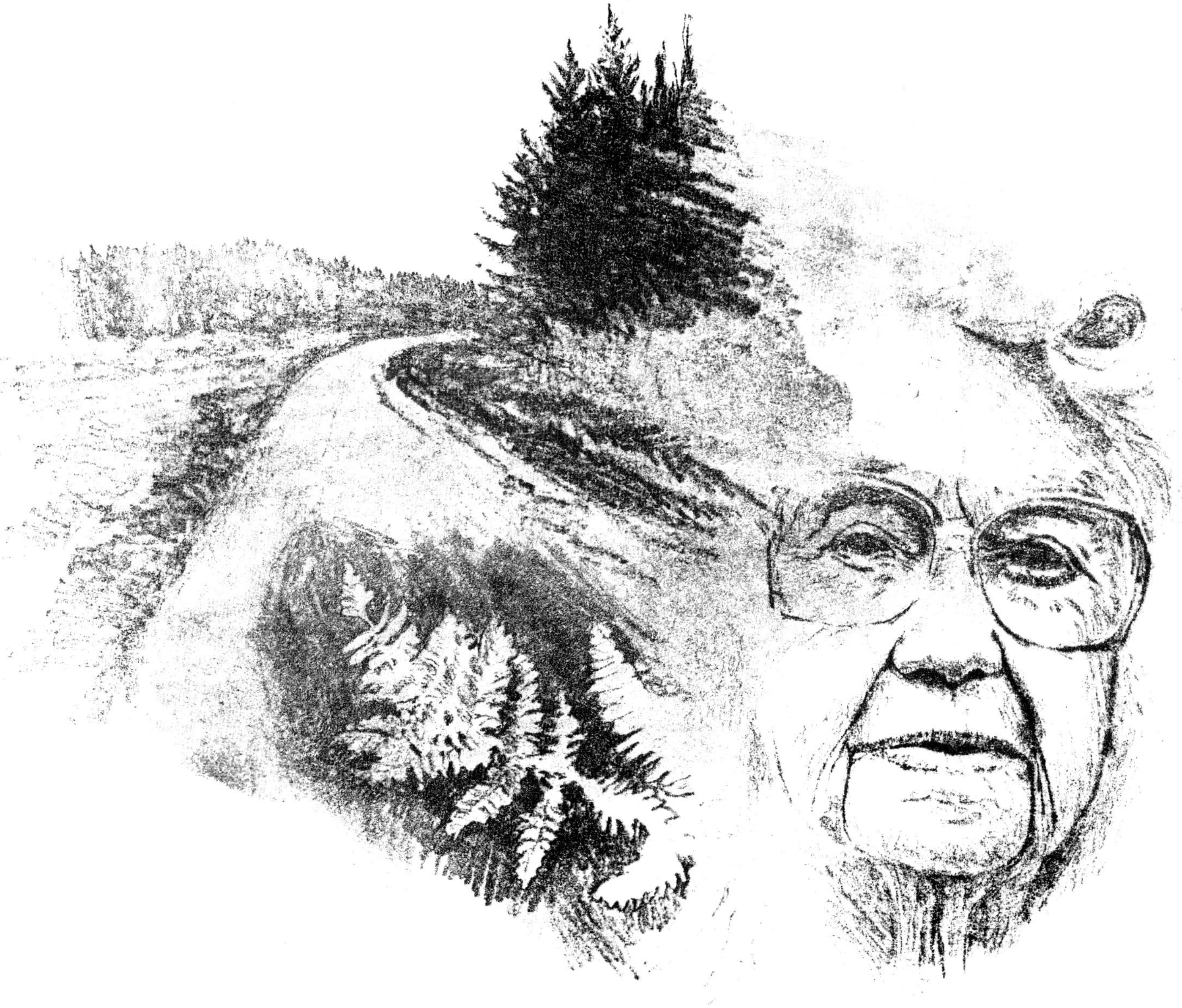

Ida was born in Alpha, Washington in 1898. When she was three her family loaded their belongings in a covered wagon and moved to Long Valley, Idaho.

"I don't have any memory of the wagon trip," says Ida, "but well I remember where we landed. We had a log cabin with a dirt floor and the winters in Long Valley were cold and the snow would pile up.

"The people who lived there before us had run out of hay and the cattle chewed the stanchion logs. I used to hate to go in to gather eggs. How the cows and calves must have suffered!

"When I was 14 I started going with Willard. He was a buckaroo, seven years older than me, and Mother warned me he was a harem-scarem type, too wild for me. One day Willard told me, 'I gotta be movin' on. You can come with me if you want, honey. If you do we'll get married.' And so I ran away from home to be with Willard.

"We made it to Weiser, Idaho, looked up the justice of the peace. I knew he would ask my age and didn't want to lie, so I had written the number 18 on a slip of paper and put it in my shoe. When he asked I told him, 'I'm over 18,' and that was good enough for him.

"We left town on the first train 'cause we figured my folks would be a'looking for us and spent the night at the Western Hotel in Nyssa, Oregon. Next day Willard caught on with a hay crew working in the fields for a dollar a day.

"I was just a green kid. Willard taught me everything; taught me to cook, scrub clothes and things like that. I loved him and he loved me.

"After harvest we took a homestead on Succor Creek in Malheur Country, lived in a 10 by 12 tent. The first month I killed 17 rattlesnakes around the tent. We had a small iron stove, a table, three wood apple boxes for chairs, some more boxes piled on top of each other for cupboards and an iron bed and spring mattress. That was it. We lived like that for two and a half years before we built. I wrote a book about our ordeal, *Our Homestead in the Canyon*.

"After a dozen years of trying to scratch out a living we gave up, sold to a cattleman and moved as far west as we could, to Florence, Oregon.

"In 1929 we bought this property here on Old Stage Coach Road. We rented a truck and a driver for the move, loaded everything we owned on it. There wasn't much of a road at the time so the driver was following the beach. We warned him it was hazardous driving too close to the water, but he didn't listen. He got a little too close, tipped the truck on its side and all we could do was watch as the tide came in and took all our household goods and clothing, every stick of furniture including my pride and joy, a player piano.

"The Coast Guard boys said the last time they saw the piano it was out playing on the ocean waves. They thought their humor was a whole lot funnier than I did. The only thing we were able to salvage was one tin cup that washed ashore when the tide changed.

"Forget Succor Creek, this here is the home place. Willard and I wore out our backs, and the kids did, too, trying to make a go of it. Tough to earn a living during the Depression. We cut

greenery, huckleberries and ferns, and sent them to a florist in Washington. He used them to make sprays.

"We finally had to work out. Both of us caught on with the school district. I was head cook, janitor and clerk. Willard drove school bus.

"Really I don't have regrets about settling here. The only regret I have is the road. December 11, 1955, Willard swerved to miss a rock and we went over the edge. I was in such bad shape they waited until just before Christmas to tell me Willard was gone. Didn't think I would pull through but I did.

"Anymore I live in my wheelchair, that's no fun, but I keep busy. Most of my family lives in houses on the property. There's grandkids and great-grandkids and great-greats. And I collect things. It would be easier to say what I don't collect than what I do. I collect plates, cups, saucers, little mementos from the old days, old-timey pictures....

"What I like to collect best of all are pens. Lot of 'em don't even look like they would write. Got a pen you would swear was an ice cream cone, another looks like a bracelet, got one like a pretzel and one like a tube of toothpaste. Got pens representing all fifty states with extras of some. Did a lot of writing to get these pens. Longest one I have is 12 full inches. My favorite is my Pacific Princess pen. Its upper half is filled with water and inside is a little tiny ship that floats back and forth when you tilt it.

"Wrote to President Reagan, asking for a pen, and he didn't even have the decency to answer. I'm gonna write and tell him not to bother running again 'cause I won't vote for him.... Just kidding.

"When President Reagan was shot and in the hospital I sent him a copy of my book, *Our Homestead in the Canyon*, so he would have something to read. He sent me a real nice letter. No pen, but he did send a letter. Got it right here. 'Thank you for sharing the inscribed copy of your book with us. We look forward to enjoying it now and shall retain it for inclusion in our future presidential collection. We sincerely appreciate your thoughtfulness and we send our best wishes to you. Nancy and Ronald Reagan.' Now, ain't that nice?"

ETHYL PARISH

Ethyl Parish sits on a lawn chair in the shade of a towering fir tree. She is holding a photograph of her late husband Ellis in her lap and dabbing at tears with a handkerchief.

"Sorry," she apologizes as she fights to regain her composure, "but it was three years ago today I lost Ellis. God bless his ol' heart...."

She dabs at her eyes again. "I remember him standing there beside me on the day we were married, September 16th, 1919. Afterward we came up here to the ranch and lived with Ellis's father. I called him Grandpa. He called me Girlie.

"Grandpa was an old man. I took care of him for his last ten years. I remember one time he told me, 'You stay here, Girlie, take care of me and I'll give you kids the ranch.' And that's exactly what he did. He died over there on that flat rock by the edge of the yard. Sat down and died. That was it.

"See this here fir tree? Sent off for it shortly after Grandpa died. Got it in the mail. Just a little bitty seedling. Planted it. Carried water to it in a bucket. Nursed it along and would you look at it now.

14

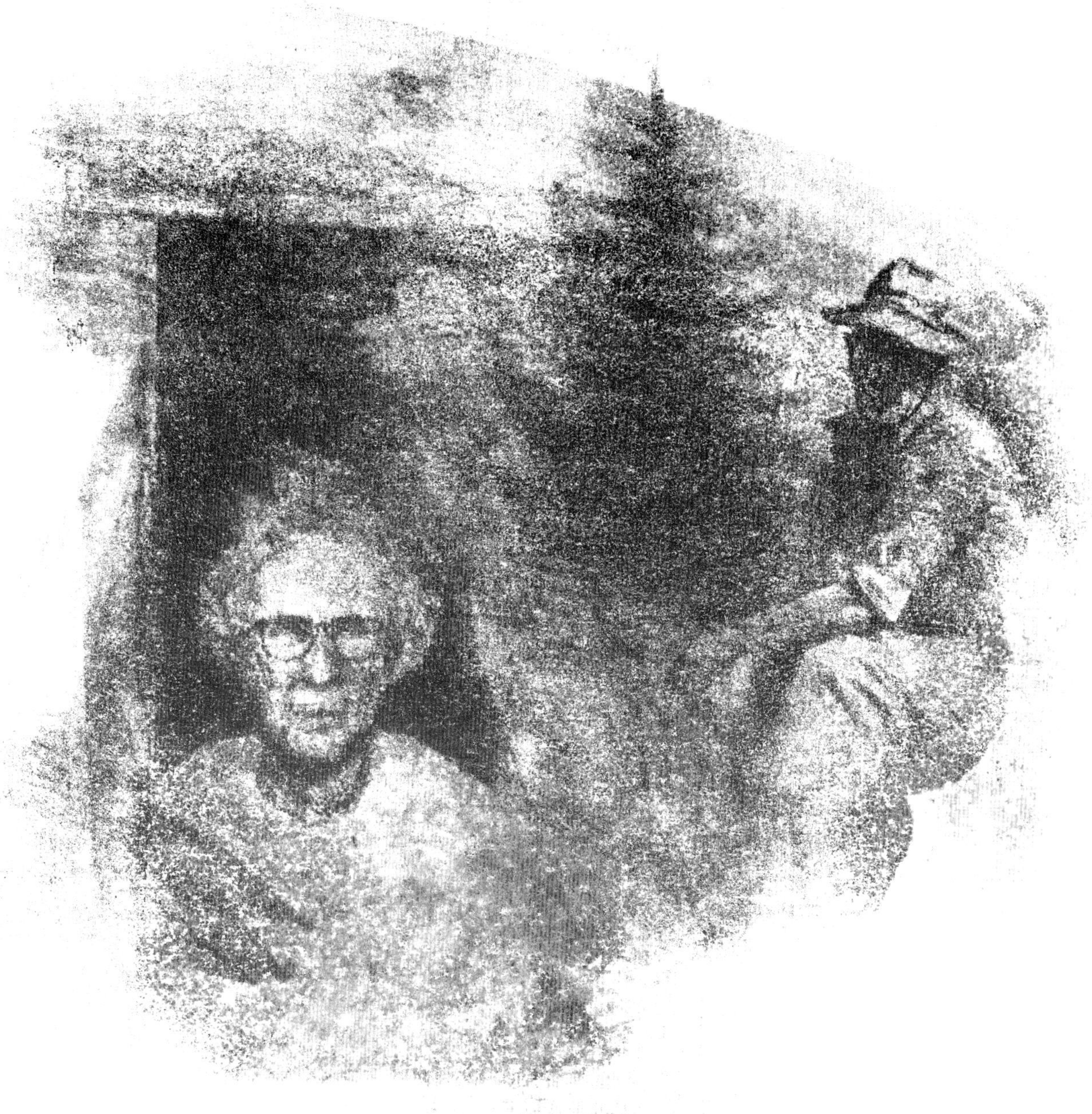

"We used to have a swing, on that branch right there, when the kids were home. Ellis and I had four boys and a girl and I've got, let's see, 15 grandkids and six great-grandkids of my own, but all the kids around this part of the country call me Grandma.

"In my lifetime I've made 132 quilts. Gave most away. Did it for something to do.

"I've lived in this house 65 years. Only times I was gone were the 23 summers we spent in a canvas-covered trailer. Ellis surveyed from Mountain Home, Idaho to Owyhee, Oregon because it had never been done before. I trailed along with him.

"Like I said, God bless his ol' heart. Ellis sure loved his horses. We always had horses. He had one horse named Tony that could count. He would paw the ground. Ellis would show off, have Tony count people's ages. Tony would count just as long as Ellis touched his side. Most folks would never catch on to the trick, not in a million years.

"Oh, Ellis could teach a horse about anything. When I think about him, and I think about him all the time, I remember him with the horses. Another thing I remember is the way he could sing and recite poems. He was a good singer. His poems, he could go on and on and never repeat himself, would tickle me so.

"Every one of the days we had together were good. Can't think of a single time we exchanged cross words.

"The day I lost him he rototilled the garden. Came in and said, 'I'm awful dirty, Mom, but I need to lie down a minute. Can I lie on the bed?'

"I told him, 'Sure you can, Sweetheart.' We talked like that to each other.

"Later on we went down to Elba to get the mail, came home and Ellis sat down in the shade of my fir tree, sat down right about here where I'm sitting, said, 'Momma, could you get me something cool to drink?' I said, 'Sure, Sweetheart,' went inside and came out with a glass of lemonade. When I got here he was gone. Happened just that fast. Bless his dear ol' heart.

"A few months ago I finally sold Tony. Got $1,500 for him. He was always Ellis's favorite.

"It's not an easy thing to do, live by yourself. If my eyes were good I wouldn't care so much, but they're bad. My arthritis bothers me quite a bit. The kids keep wanting me to take turns living a few months with each of them but I'm going to stay in this house as long as I can. I'll tough it out this year at least. This is home. This is where the memories...."

BRIDGE MALEY

Bridge Maley brings in a big armload of firewood and dumps it in the wood box. He peels off his gloves and lays them aside.

"All my life I worked in the woods, worked hard falling timber. In the early days I pulled a seven-foot cross-cut saw. The first gas-fired saw I used was a Timber Hauler, weighed 135 pounds and took two men to operate. Put in 38 years. And then along came the 17th of December, 1981. That's a date etched in my mind.

"Was working for Murphy Logging up the Middle Fork of the Willamette. Started off like any other day. Up early, got to the job at daybreak. Cold, maybe 10 degrees, spitting snow. Was packing my saw, gas and oil up a snowbank when a pain hit me full in the chest. Only way I can describe it is to say it felt like an anvil sitting on top of me. Started to sweat. Left arm numb. Hard to breathe. Sick to my stomach. Had to sit down.

"I took a 15-minute blow, felt a little better. Thought maybe I had a bout of the flu. Told myself I had worked feeling worse. Convinced myself of it.

"Fell timber all day. Came home and didn't mention what happened to the wife. That evening my daughter had a basketball game and I felt I should go. Didn't get home until about 10:30. Went to the shop to sharpen my saw. Had another little episode where my arm went dead and my chest hurt. Didn't really know what to think. Crawled in bed and along about two in the morning I woke up with pain in my chest. This time it was worse. Shook Toby, my wife, awake and told her she better run me to the hospital.

"Six months before all this happened I had taken a physical and the doctor told me I had the heart of a 20-year-old. Said my lifetime of hard work had me in the peak of condition. Never thought hard work could kill a fellow.

19

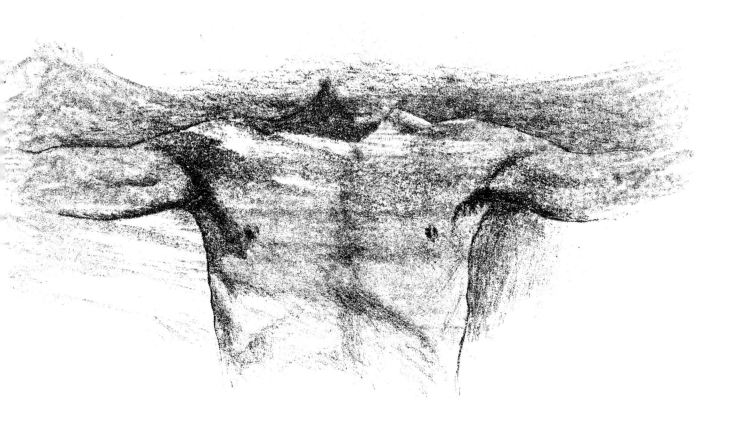

"At the hospital the doctor told me I had survived a massive heart attack and that 30% of my heart was gone. I couldn't believe it.

"Kept me eight days in intensive care and another week in the hospital. Sent me home and I was pretty disillusioned because I knew I would never fall timber again and didn't know how much a man could do with a chunk of his heart missing. After a while I realized the 70% I still had was plenty. Did exactly what the doctors told me to do, took the medicine and limited my physical activity, although every day I tried to do a little more. When I proved to myself there were some good years in front of me I went back to the doctor and told him I wanted off the medicine.

"He gave me the treadmill test and I was still going when he shut it down, said any man with the stamina I had did not need medication. Told me to take an aspirin a day and that was all.

"I'm officially retired, do pretty much what I want. Fish, cut firewood, piddle around. Took up a new hobby — golf. Chase that little white ball around the course three or four times a week. On the side I repair golf clubs.

"I'm living proof a heart attack doesn't have to stop you in your tracks. The way I look at it, if the good Lord wants me, He's going to have to catch me on the run."

21

BABE MCVAY

"Was born up ta Spokane, Washington, back in '04. The summer of '17 we pulled stakes, left that country in a covered wagon," recalled Millard "Babe" McVay.

"We had a pretty fair load 'cause we had all our personal belongin's, everythin' we owned. Dad had built a couple of cages on the back of the wagon, brought a little red sow and the chickens. Had fresh eggs ta eat if we could get 'em 'fer they broke.

"Twenty-three days on the road. Camped under the stars. Cooked over an open fire. Come through Horse Heaven ta the Columbia River. They was just buildin' the road 'long the north side an' it was next ta impassable. But we made 'er.

"Dad went ta loggin' in the Cascades an' we lived in loggin' camps. When school come 'round I had ta ride horseback five miles, ta the last barn, hoof it from there another mile. There wasn't no barn at school an' ya don't wanna leave a horse out in the weather.

"Got my eighth grade diploma. Figured that was enough, took off ta work in the woods. Chased all over these hills. Started in buckin' logs with a misery whip. No power saws back then.

Worked my way up ta high climber. First tree I climbed was a little fellar. Kept at it, 'fore long was goin' up over a hundred feet. No room fer mistakes. Gotta tend ta business. Mistake'll kill ya.

"Never one ta be bashful 'bout spendin' money. Bought a 1919 Buick, almost new. I was but a pup, 16 years old. After that I had a Maxwell but wrecked it, run it into a tree and tore the top off. After that bought a Nash convertible 'bout the time the Depression really hit. Got laid off. Went ta Eastern Washington, worked in the harvest. Made it through the summer in fair shape. Came home an' didn't do much of nothin' that winter 'cept run a trap line. Caught coon, rats an' a few mink. Quite a lotta coon.

"When the woods opened went back ta loggin' camp and stuck with it after that. In '40 I started my own show. Bought a little steam donkey. Bought five forties laid 'tween Deadwood

23

and Lake Creek. Had a sawmill. Done it all with the help of one fellar. Him an' me got along good.

"Back in them days I used ta do a little fightin'. One time I got in a fight at the grange hall dance an' this fellar, his name was Sy Harpold, he bites off my ear! Lose an ear an' I guarantee ya it sure can hurt for a little thin'. Anyways, a local promoter arranged a grudge match 'tween Sy and me. Suppose ta fight six rounds. He didn't last but three. Knocked 'im out.

"Promoter thought I was a pretty good bet. Lined me up fer three professional fights. Won the first two. Lost the last. That was it. Didn't wanna fight in the ring no more.

"Had a pretty good career in the woods. Made some money. Spent a lot. Got married in '34. Same gal, still married.

"I'm supposed ta be retired. They tell me I am, but I ain't sure. Hazel an' I winter in California, at Desert Hot Springs. That's the poor man's Palm Springs.

"First year down there I trimmed the palm trees on our property. Then the neighbors asked me ta trim theirs. A lot of 'em are pretty well ta do and they don't mind payin' cash. Business took off. Was more busy'n unbusy.

"Best days of my life were spent strapped in spurs. The worst, too. Fell outta trees two different times, both were palm trees.

"First was in '84. Buggered up my back, laid me out fer a few weeks. Eighty years old ya don't heal quite as quick.

"Second time was the big one. That was in '85. Had my belt on, everythin' goin' good, an' the snap breaks. Never heard of a snap breakin'. Good belt, too. Won it in a high climbin' contest at the fair in '56. Shouldn't of broke. But it did. Fell

maybe thirty feet onto an asphalt roadway. Broke an arm, two ribs an' my pelvis, punctured a lung an' this shoulder had ta be sewed up. Doctor, he sees me, says, 'Oh no, not you again!'

"Folks tell me I oughta give 'er up, quit climbin'. But I ain't agonna. I'll be a high climber 'til the day I die."

PONDEROSA PINE

CHAPTER 2

The ponderosa pine is a tall, stately tree which typifies the unconquered spirit and the open spaces of the West. Growing in park-like stands on sunny mountain slopes and high plateaus, ponderosa pine sinks roots deep into volcanic soil, tapping into the 15 or so inches of annual moisture while its branches seek out the sun.

Cap Collier spent his working career logging the great pine forest east of the Cascade mountain range. He witnessed the technological revolution in logging. Cap's legacy is preserved in the land and his collection of outdated logging equipment he donated to the state of Oregon for a logging museum and park.

The straight grain of the western pine has many uses, one of them for carving. Because of failing health Martha Shelley can no longer work with horses as she loved to do, so she spends her remaining years whittling horses.

Del Brock knows about the various qualities of the woods he uses to handcraft guitars and violins; maple, spruce, pine, each has its own character. He has a sixth sense, an ability to look inside the texture of the wood and know what sound it will produce. And when he fits the pieces together into what he calls "a happy family", new life is created from scraps of dead wood.

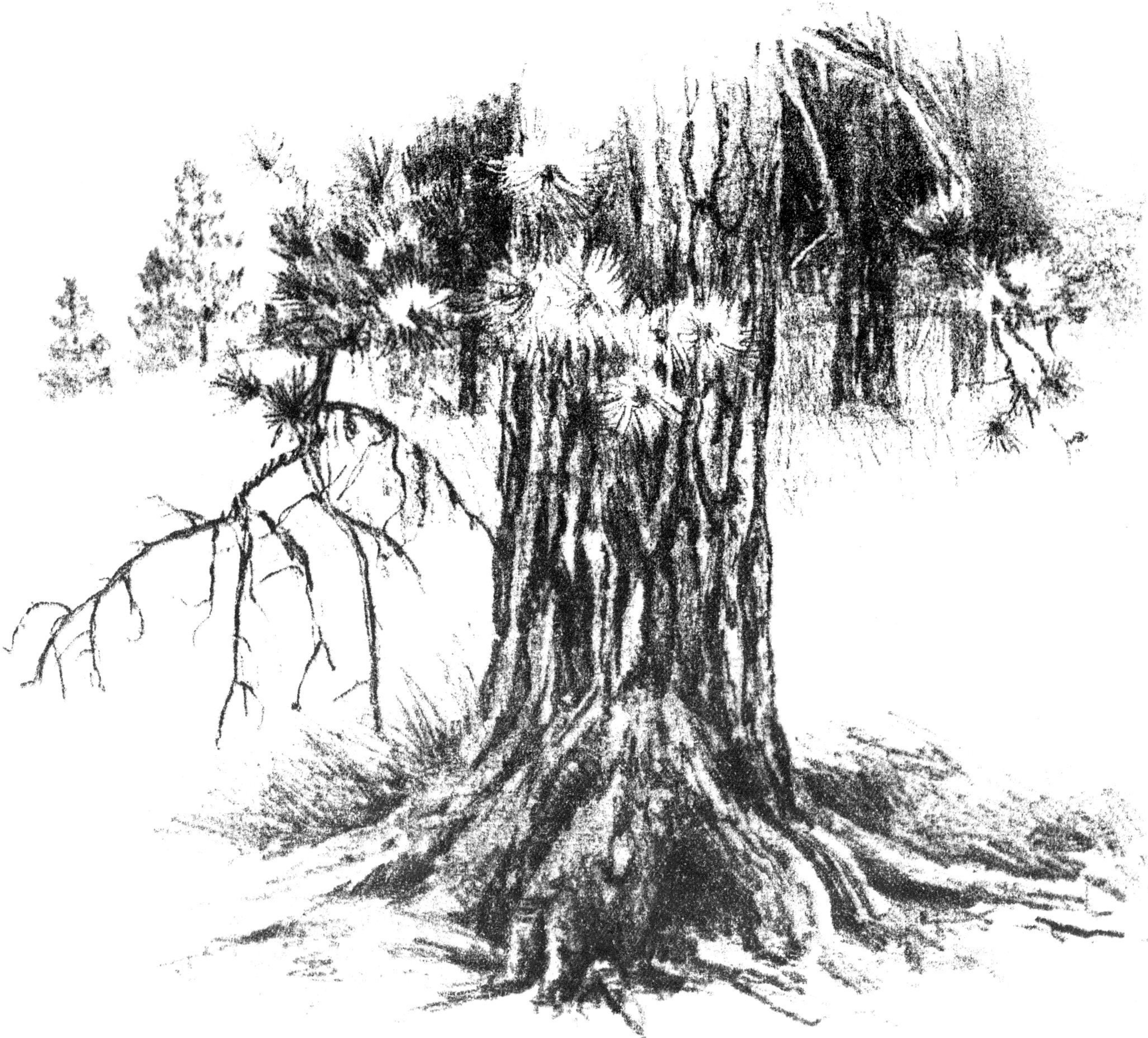

LONE PINE

Three hundred years ago, in the southern end of the Kittitas Valley, a solitary ponderosa pine tree took root near a spring that bubbled forth and fed a marsh where beaver and muskrat lived. Ducks and geese dropped in to rest and feed. At night frogs croaked and crickets chirped. Indians, following the trail between the Columbia River and Snoqualmie Pass, occasionally camped at the spring.

Clark Runyan, who has lived on the Lone Pine Ranch for the past 30 years, says, "I drained the swamp, made it into a nice field. I know that Indians used to camp beneath the lone pine because my plow has turned up arrowheads and obsidian flakes.

"Some of the old-timers told me that back in the 1870s, during the Indian uprising, the homesteaders in this area built a blockhouse for protection near the lone pine. But I've never found any evidence of it.

"I was also told a horse thief was strung up in the tree. I think they probably used the big limb that comes straight out. It seems like the kind of a limb a lynch party would throw a rope over.

"The original homestead must have been nearby because there were still a few twisted apple trees scattered around. I pulled them out. That's about all I know."

If the lone pine could talk it would tell about the comings and goings of the Indians, about the first trappers and traders into the country, about the cattlemen, the pioneers and the homesteaders. Its life has spanned the history of the white man in the Kittitas Valley. Now age has laid claim to it and it is slowly dying.

CAP COLLIER

"I'll tell you this up front. My park has the largest collection of logging equipment anywhere in the world. Come on, I'll show you around," said ninety-year-old Alfred "Cap" Collier. He shuffles off down a well-worn path that weaves its way across a flat of sagebrush and pine trees.

After going a short distance Cap says, "Let's take a breather." He leans back against a tree and begins to tell the history leading to the creation of Collier Memorial State Park, located in the heart of a ponderosa pine forest thirty-five miles north of Klamath Falls, Oregon.

"I was born in the Willamette Valley back in 1892, December 14th. Came over the hill when I was a young man. All this was open country then. No fences. No roads. Very few people.

"One time I rode horseback to Crater Lake. After a long pull, where I had to lead my horse, I topped out and what a magnificent view it was! I think the lake was even more beautiful back then. The blue was bluer. I spent an entire day rolling rocks. The water was so clear the rocks could be seen tumbling end over end for I don't know how many hundred feet. Though I went back to Crater Lake, lots of times since then, I never rolled any more rocks. Guess I had my fill.

"Better keep moving," says Cap and he leads the way down the path. Stopping frequently he tells the history of everything in sight, all of it logging equipment: stiff booms, log loaders, a cross-cut power saw, steam donkeys, a solid wooden-wheeled cart pulled by oxen, a wood-burning locomotive which he says had the nickname G.O.P. because the passengers and crew were often requested to Get Out and Push. "She was used in the redwoods, down near Mt. Shasta," he says, "at the turn of the century."

Cap shows off a blacksmith shed that is completely equipped with a forge, anvil, bellows, harness and yokes, even a sling to raise up draft horses to facilitate shoeing. Then it is on to a homestead cabin, a museum within a museum. On display in the cabin are a wide variety of hand tools and artifacts: peaveys, felling axes, harness, a drafting table, kerosene lamps, a tobacco plug cutter....

"Early on I went to work in the woods," tells Cap. "Spent my whole life in the timber business.

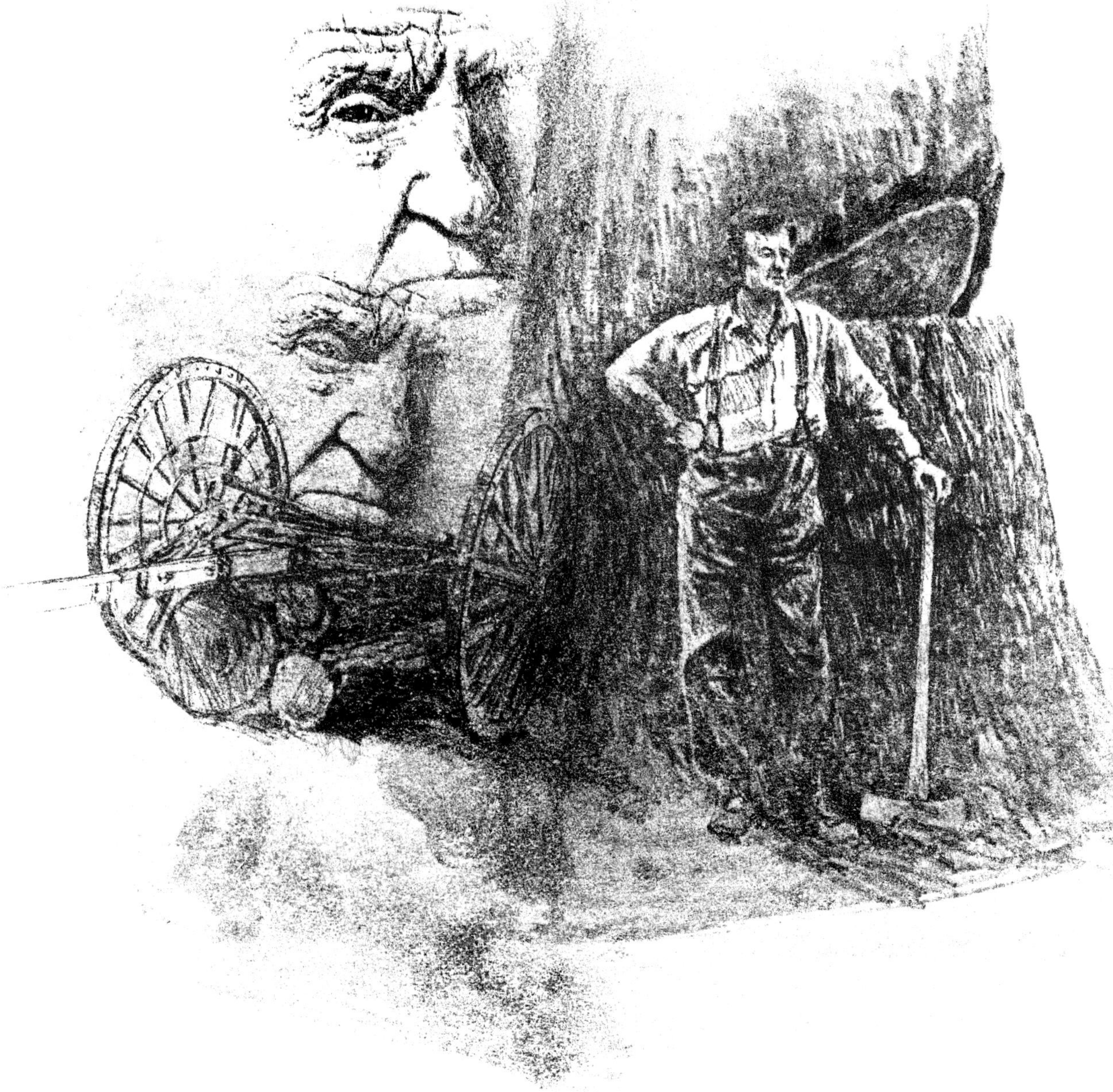

"I was witness to a whole spectrum of change. From ax and misery whip and logging with oxen to steam power saws, donkeys and locomotives. And then the gas engine took over and the steam engine became obsolete. I saw it all.

"In 1945 my brother Andrew, he was in the business, too, and I decided to donate this land to the state of Oregon as a memorial to our parents (Charles and Janet Collier). We did it for a couple of reasons. First of all, this land is something special. With Spring Creek and the Williamson River running through it, this is as pretty a place as I ever found. The way things are going I wanted to make sure there would always be one spot on earth where a poor man can go fishing when he wants. The only stipulation we made when we gave the land to the state was that they can never charge a fee to set foot here.

"As far as the museum goes, well that came about kind of natural. I had my own logging machinery and my brother had some and, of course, friends made donations. We loaded up the place with equipment. When we turned it over there was probably a half-million dollars worth of equipment here and we've added to it."

Cap leads the way to the most eye-catching pieces of logging equipment, the high-wheels, aptly named because of their ten-foot tall, wooden-spoked, metal-rimmed wheels. They were used to move logs from the forest to the landing. Cap comments, "Tourists take thousands of pictures standing here in front of these. Most have never seen anything like it in their lives and have a hard time believing high-wheels were actually used in logging. But they were."

Cap goes to where a section of a giant log is protected by a roof. "This is the Clatsop Fir, the world's largest Douglas fir. It was brought over from the coast. You read the plaque."

The plaque gives the particulars on the tree, stating it was toppled by high winds on November 25, 1962. The stump was 15' 6" in diameter and the height, with a broken top, was 200' 6". The volume of the tree was estimated at more than 100,000 board feet, enough to build ten two-bedroom houses.

Cap steps to the sawed section of the log where the growth rings can be clearly seen. He points to a spot near the outer rim of bark and says, "Right about there was when I was born." His finger moves inward passing a hundred more rings, wide rings indicating good growth years and narrow rings from when the rains did not come. He states, "Right about here Robert Gray discovered the Columbia River and about here the Colonies broke away from Great Britain. Here Christopher Columbus landed on the North American continent. They say the Vikings came first but I don't know about that. And right here in the center, at this time in history, Marco Polo was traveling across China. Seven hundred years ago this tree was a seedling.

"I'm an old man. I've seen a lot of changes. Yes, I have. I come here, stand by this log, and I put time in perspective.

"It gives me peace of mind to know that this park and museum will be here for those who come this way, for all time. That is what I leave this world. Collier Park. Treat it well."

37

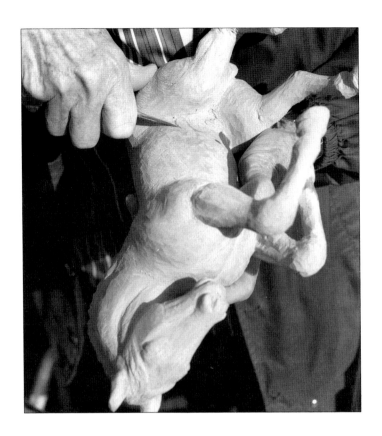

MARTHA SHELLEY

Martha Shelley deftly rolls a block of pine wood in her hands, using a pocketknife to take out a gouge here, a sliver there, continually rolling and working the wood. She whittles and visits.

"I was born 'long the Alsea River, 1895. Mother had asthma and the damp weather was bad on her health so Father traded the place for a wheat ranch in eastern Oregon.

"We moved in 1898. I remember it was a long way. Mother drove a four-horse team pullin' a wagon with a hack fastened in tandem. Father drove six horses pulling two regular farm wagons hooked tandem.

"Our new home was out from Heppner. When we got there my twin sister looks 'round at those dry ol' hills and says, 'There ain't nothin' grows 'round here.'

"Our nearest neighbor was five miles away. The Indians were our playmates. We did have a church in the neighborhood. Once a month a preacher would come 'round and take care of the marryin' and buryin'.

"I remember one time a neighbor went into hock to buy twelve head of purebred Herefords. A terrific lightnin' storm come through, hit the fence and killed all twelve 'cause they had their heads stretched 'tween wires, tryin' to get at some grass.

"On June 14, 1903 I was witness to one of the great tragedies in Oregon's history. The sky got a deep navy blue. Not black, navy blue. Lightnin' like you've never seen. Thunder boomin' all 'round. And then it began to rain, and it rained, and rained. We sat there on the porch and watched it all.

"Rain slacked off a bit and that was when the wall of water come down a gully off Balm Fork. The chickens went a runnin', course they couldn't outrun the water. It swept 'em away. It went on down and all but wiped Heppner off the map. Nearly 300 people were killed.

"That was the first time I ever experienced fear. Never again could I watch thunderheads boil up over the Blue Mountains and think they were beautiful.

"In my whole life my father never once gave me, or any of his kids, a toy. Instead he gave us horses. My first horse was Kit. I was maybe five or six. Father bought him from a sheepherder. He was nothin' but an open-range horse but he had fine bloodlines, slim bones and was gentle as a house cat. Father set me on his back, led me 'round the corral a time or two, handed me the reins and said, 'He's all yours.'

"Father had a real love for horses. Mostly he kept pureblood Clydesdales. He said they were intelligent and easy to teach. One thing he told me was to never buy a fat horse 'cause you can't see the bone structure. Said to compare the front half and the back half an' make sure they match up. He taught me a lot of other things, too. Everythin' I know.

"It was a horse finally did in Father. He was ridin' a colt up in the rimrock. Colt spooked, maybe it was a rattlesnake, reared and went over. The doctor said when Father hit, a blood vessel ruptured in his heart. That was it. Didn't have a father no more.

"I've had heart trouble myself, in 1959 had a doozey of a heart attack. Was off my feet, flat on my back, in bed, for four months. Doctor told me I was gonna have to quit horses. Was trainin' horses at the time. Felt like tellin' him, 'That's what you think, buster,' but didn't say nothin' at all.

40

"Turned out, in a way, he was right and in a way I was right. Never went back to workin' horses but for therapy I started whittlin' and it's progressed from there...."

The horses Martha carves are put in her House of Horses Museum, a building behind her rural home. She flips on a set of overhead lights illuminating a series of shadow boxes lining the walls and spilling over into the center of the room. Shadow boxes filled with hand-carved horses.

"My grandparents came to Oregon over the Oregon Trail in 1847," Martha tells. "Mother was born before Oregon even became a state...."

Each display depicts another segment of life before the advent of the automobile. Horses pull a stagecoach, horses pull a loaded freight wagon, a cowboy rides a bucking horse, wild horses run over a hill....

Martha points to a shadow box with a single horse pulling a cutter and says, "The night Mike proposed to me we were ridin' in a cutter exactly like this one. He's been gone 16 years now...."

m door on her way out and uses a
kes her way down the trail leading
ol in the kitchen and automatically
years old. I'm doin' what I wanna
ad, don't know why I can't go on
reath. That would suit me fine."

FRANK KING

Tucked away in an isolated corner of Idaho was a beautiful
forested valley. No roads led into the area. It was crossed only
by game trails and visited by Indians from the nearby mission
of Desmet who came to hunt deer in the thick, pine forest.

44

One day in 1910 Calvin King, a sharecropper from North Carolina, wandered into this wilderness valley after having ridden horseback for fifty miles. The day before, in Coeur d'Alene, he had drawn a number in a homestead lottery. He had taken a gambler's chance and now, surveying the land, he knew he had won. The soil was rich, deep and well-watered. This valley was beyond his highest expectations. Here he would carve a home for his family. But the big trees and the tangle of underbrush would have to be cleared before it could be farmed. Calvin returned to town to gather his wife Lunar and their seven children.

Seventy years later, in a neat white house perched on the crown of a small hill, lives the last of the King family, Calvin's son Frank. From his vantage on the porch Frank surveys the fields, the ground plowed and freshly disced. Within a week grain will be planted and soon the rich black soil will take on the green hue of winter wheat. King Valley. Frank helped create it. He cleared the towering pine trees, cut the brush and turned the virgin soil. His whole life has been spent here.

"When we came we lived in a tent, over there," says Frank, pointing toward a small timbered island on the valley floor. "Dad cut down the big trees and us kids cleared brush. Lordy, the brush was thick, just a tangle. By fall we had a log cabin to live in.

"Dad and the neighbors built a school on the lower corner of our property. Every morning, on the way to school, us kids worked cutting brush until the school bell rang. On the way home we worked until suppertime. There wasn't time for fun and play.

46

"We fell the big trees, some were sold to a sawmill but most were burned. The stumps we either pulled or farmed around until they rotted. The brush was piled into huge piles and we had bonfires. I well remember the wood smoke, it lay like a fog over the valley.

"There were folks on every 160 acres but the living was hard, one by one they abandoned their homesteads. We bought land as it became available, sometimes paying just a few dollars an acre, until the King family was the only one left. We owned it all. King Valley.

"The other kids in the family moved away, too, but I stayed. I couldn't leave it. This place is in my blood.

"Come March I'll be 80 years old. Anymore I rest my bones. No more clearing, no more farming, no more caring for stock. I lease out the farm ground. And I made six home sites. Six families live here. They're good company. Treat me fine. Here a while back they went together and bought me a gold-braided cap says King Valley, Idaho, and a new pair of overalls with a patch says King of King Valley. Made me laugh.

"I sit here, look out over this valley, gives me some pride knowing I helped clear it, helped put it into production. This ground grows some of the best grain in the world. Yes it does.

"I know that I'm not going to live forever. No one does. Before I go I'd like to put up a monument on the home place. Nothing big, just enough to let folks know it was the King family who settled here, the King family who broke out the land."

DEL BROCK

Del Brock sits on a round of pine, amid a pile of firewood, and his strong, hardworking fingers trace the delicate outline of the violin; the back, sides and neck of fiddleback maple, the top — the heart — of Engelman spruce. He cut the spruce in the Lochsa River canyon, near his home in Lowell, Idaho, and allowed it to cure for twelve long years before he ever touched it.

He tucks the instrument under his chin, draws the bow across the strings and as the melody flows, the wood comes to life, its music bittersweet, sad.

Del was born on a farm in Iowa, the son of a poor sharecropper. At the age of four he picked up a harmonica for the first time and astounded his parents by playing *Yankee Doodle Dandy*. That Christmas Santa Claus brought him a ukulele, and the next year he received an inexpensive guitar.

Del remembers, "I had a knack for woodworking and knew I could make a better guitar than the one I had. Gave it a try and, by gosh, the one I built sounded better. Then the neighbors started bringing me broken instruments to fix. I learned a lot from seeing how they were put together and before long I was so busy making guitars and violins I didn't have time to play. But I didn't mind."

Del lays the violin on his lap, comments, "Five of my violins are being played in philharmonic orchestras. I could name a dozen top country bands that have a Brock guitar. Take pride in my work. Never wanted to be average. Always wanted to be the best.

"I'm a throwback to another age, an age before mass production, when musical instruments were carved by loving hands. Each wood has special musical properties. I cut the piece to fit with exact tolerance and make sure each piece blends with the properties of the other wood. Together they make what I call the family, and like a family all must work together in harmony. If they do not, then the family suffers.

"I don't work for money. I'm lucky to make minimum wage. Never have charged what the market will bear. Try to keep the price where a poor man can afford to buy. Keeps me busy. Don't have to advertise. All been word of mouth. Only stipulation is my customer must be serious about music.

"As soon as someone picks up an instrument I can tell if they really love to play. If they do then I work it out so they can afford one of my violins or guitars."

Del talks about music and his life. His eight-year-old son, Jason, comes outside and plays with the dog. Del watches him, says wistfully, "He came along a little late in life. I'm 64 years old. Married a woman 18 years younger than me. She is my second wife. Kids from my first marriage are all grown.

"See a lot of myself in Jason. I was always a bit of a Huck Finn. Only hope the good Lord spares me time to raise him."

Last fall Del was sick and knew something was wrong. He visited the veteran's hospital and doctors diagnosed lymphatic cancer. It was so advanced no treatment could be given. They told Del he had no more than two years to live.

"When the doctors told me, I was stunned. Why me? I've always been a Christian man, believed in God, believed in heaven. Hit me hard. Then it dawned on me we are all living under a time limit. Mine might be shorter than most but I decided, okay, I'll take those two years and make them ten."

Jason wanders over and sits beside Del. Del hesitates a moment, looking at the violin in his hands. He wants to say this is the best violin he ever made, that it is the culmination of a lifetime of sculpting violins; but emotions choke him. Instead he hands the violin to Jason, tells him, "Son, this is my last violin. The last one I'll be able to make. I want you to have it."

Jason accepts it and then he tells his father, "Dad, I know you're sick. I know you're not kidding me. I know you are going to die. But someday I'm going to die, too. And then we can be in heaven, together."

The tears come. His last violin. Last violin....

THE WILLOW

CHAPTER 3

Willows are found throughout the West but mainly along rivers and streams and wherever springs boil up or moisture collects. They help stabilize stream banks and provide shade for fish as well as cover and food for many birds and animals. In winter they contribute a splash of color; yellow, orange or red, and are the first to signal the coming of spring when catkins appear on pussy willows in advance of the leaves.

Clarence Nuxoll attests to the willow's ability to take root and grow quickly. As a boy he pushed a willow switch into the ground. A half century later Clarence remains firmly rooted, farming the home place, and the willow switch is a magnificent tree.

The three Bengoa brothers and their families live clustered under one roof and work together to maintain a sprawling ranch, eighty miles down a dirt road from the nearest outpost of civilization.

In the West the best grass grows along the willow-lined streams that meander across meadows. Ross Plummer tried his hand at many professions but the one he kept coming back to was stock raising. And now in old age, though he lives in town, every evening he walks to the city limits and watches the horses graze in the meadow. Each visit ignites a lifetime of memories and those are enough to sustain him.

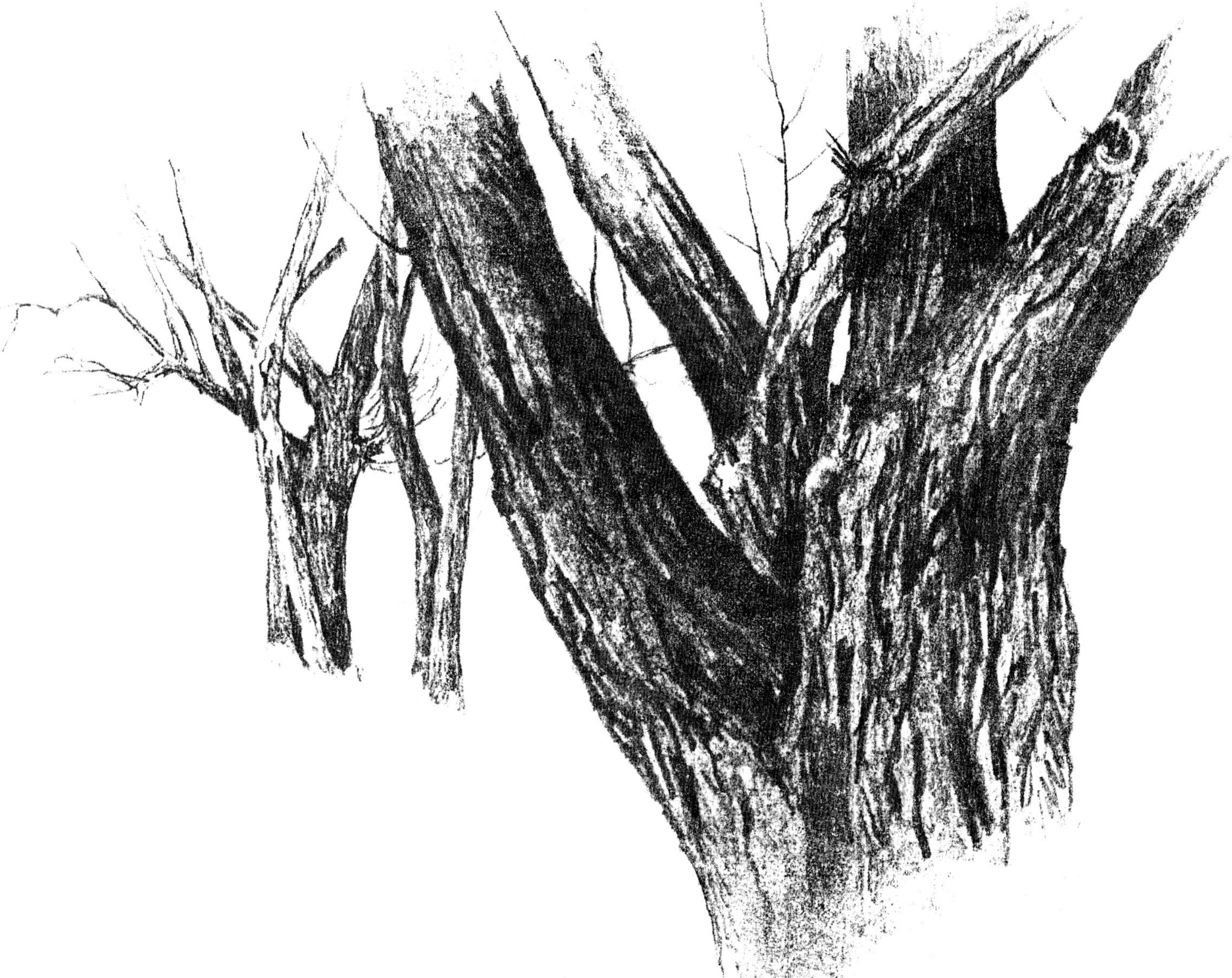

CLARENCE NUXOLL

Clarence Nuxoll holds an obsidian spearpoint in his hand and says, "Found this in the mud, up by the spring where we get water for the house. Nez Perce Indian, I'd guess. Lots of history 'round here. Lots of history.

"My grandparents homesteaded this property back in 1895. Before that it belonged to the Indians. Dad was never anywhere but here. He's 85 years old. I do most of the work now.

"Over the years our family has built up one of the finest farm shops in the state of Idaho. Dad is the kind of fellow who always liked to see what he could build with his hands and his head. The kind of guy who takes a watch apart to see how it works. That's me, too.

"If a piece of machinery breaks down I can take a bit of scrap iron and forge a new one. Early on Dad taught me how to blacksmith. In fact, when I was a kid I made spending money making cross-links for chains. Chains were vital in the early days 'cause the roads were muddy and rough. Cross-links gave out and if you didn't fix 'em right away they'd beat a Model A to death. Stores sold cross-links for 15 cents but I bought long rods of wire and turned 'em out on a homemade machine for half a cent apiece. One year sold 10,000 links. Our mailman was my best customer.

"The folks have been married going on 60 years. We built the house they live in thirty-some-odd years ago. Went top-drawer all the way. Remember it cost $3,000 for materials.

"Doesn't seem like it was that long ago. Living out here, years kind of slide together. Lose track. Time, it marches on.

"To show you, when I was a kid I always had to go out into the pasture and bring in the cows at milking time. I never went after 'em what I didn't grab a willow switch.

"One day Mom got after me, said to put down the switch and not bother the cows with it. So I shoved it into the mud by the corner post. This big ol' tree is what it grew into."

HENRY VOGLER

Henry "Bobby" Vogler III sits at the kitchen table of the Island Ranch, sipping black coffee and telling the rich history of the Vogler clan.

"The original Henry Vogler immigrated from Germany to the United States back in the 1880s. When he landed, a group of sailors took him to a beer hall to celebrate. They stole his money and left him broke. But one thing about the Vogler family, we always come back. There's been a saying handed down from generation to generation: There's no disgrace in being broke, it's just inconvenient.

"My dad, Henry Vogler II, better known as Hank, was born in New York City in 1891. When he was about five years old the family moved west, settling first in Idaho and then moving to Eastern Washington where Granddad took a homestead and raised wheat. He bought out his neighbors whenever he had the opportunity and by the time World War I rolled around, the Voglers had quite a wheat-growing operation.

"I remember Dad telling me how they sat on four years worth of grain and when the price reached $2.50 a bushel he tried to convince his father to sell. But Granddad said they would wait, that the price would go higher.

"Dad was right, the bottom fell out of the grain market and you couldn't give it away. They lost everything, the land, the homestead, the machinery.

"When the crash hit, my folks had just got married. Mother told me she was able to borrow $200 and spent it buying a house in the town of Connell so at least they would have a place to live. She worked in a restaurant to pay off the debt.

"Dad went out and worked wherever he could find a job. He helped build the highway that ran along the Columbia River between Pendleton and Arlington. He worked in a box factory in Bend and helped build a sawmill in Westfir. He even went to California and drove snowplow in the mountains. Finally he was able to return to Connell and buy the Caterpillar tractor dealership. That was in 1926.

"Depression hit in '29. Nobody could buy new equipment

and so Dad set up a garage and fixed farmers' tractors. Mother ran a small hotel and boarding house and I swept the lodge hall and ran errands for pocket change.

"The Depression left Dad with only one piece of machinery, a Caterpillar tractor that was stored at Elk City, Idaho. There was a fire there and the lean-to where it was parked caught fire. The tractor was insured and, even though it was the dead of winter, the insurance company sent an adjuster out to settle the damages.

"Dad and the adjuster rode to Elk City horseback. On the way they passed the cabin of a moonshiner and they stopped there, decided to buy a bottle to keep them warm. The adjuster must have got warmed clean through because when he inspected the tractor he claimed it was a total loss. Dad asked if he could buy it back for parts. As it turned out all the tractor needed was a new magneto and a little paint.

"Dad took the insurance money and got back into farming. One of his favorite tricks was to buy a place in the spring, farm it, take the harvest, and sell the land. He rode the crest of a price wave and parlayed his way into owning 30,000 acres of wheat land.

"In 1945 a real estate friend brought Dad to southeast Oregon, saying he had the opportunity to sell the Island Ranch but was not sure if it was worth the price. He wanted Dad's opinion. Dad asked how much the owner wanted and bought it on the spot. He said he saw real opportunity here.

"There was a lot of work to do. We built miles of dikes, set up culverts and head gates, pumped the marshes dry and dozed out the willows. We grew barley and hay and raised cattle. At one time we had 90,000 contiguous acres and 38,000 head of cattle.

"Dad was a worker and a dreamer but he never had much interest in the business end of the operation. His system of filing was a shoe box. He spent money until he didn't have any and then he would go borrow enough to keep going.

"Since I was a freshman in high school I kept the family books. Maybe I worked too hard in the fields when I was young, but the last thing I wanted to do was farm or ranch. I wanted to be a lawyer and even graduated from college in pre-law, but instead of continuing school I came back and helped Dad run the ranch. I handled the business end of things and educated myself on taxes and laws and what you can and can't do.

"On June 3, 1973 Dad put in a full day's work overhauling a tractor. In the evening he washed the family car. And then he went over to the neighbors and was visiting when he dropped dead of a heart attack.

"I'm retired now and my son, Henry Vogler IV, we call him Little Hank even though he's six foot four, has taken over the operation. Some day, if his son, Henry Vogler V, wants to be a rancher maybe Island Ranch will be passed on to him. If he wants it."

59

JEWELLE PARMAN

Sunlight filtering through willow leaves casts a dappled pattern on the yellow legal-sized tablet in Jewelle Parman's lap. She reads aloud the words as they are written in longhand.

"Two cowboys were making camp at a lonely desert waterhole. It was the only water for miles...."

She draws a deep breath, lets it out slowly, mulling the words and her own memories of the desert. "I'm a retired cowgirl. That's all I am," she tells.

60

Jewelle knows the West as few others do. She was born in 1905 in Modoc County, California and moved with her folks to Gerlach, Nevada when she was five years old.

"We traveled in two covered wagons and, believe it or not, after we got where we were goin' we lived in tents until Dad could get around to building a house.

"I was nine years old when my father was killed. He got tangled up in a dispute with a neighbor and the neighbor shot him. Let's just say it didn't surprise me none. Dad was one mighty tough customer.

"We stayed on at the homestead. I never was one for inside work — cooking, knitting and the like. I was a tomboy, more boy than girl, that was for sure. Worked cattle, built fence, put up hay. In the winter I had to live in town, Gerlach, in order to go to school. Hated school but come spring it was back to the home place. That was where I felt I belonged.

"When I was 16 Mother allowed me to go to Reno. It was my first trip to a big city and there was a rodeo going on. Mother was so afraid I would enter the rodeo and get myself hurt she made me take a dress and leave my riding clothes at home.

"But I was a determined girl. When I got to the rodeo I borrowed a pair of boots, a riding skirt and shirt from a cowgirl and a cowboy lent me his hat. I rode in the relay race, won second place, I did, and that was against some pretty stiff competition.

61

"The best thing about the rodeo wasn't so much in finishing second — it was in meeting the famous western writer and artist, Will James. I enjoyed drawing, horses mostly, and fancied myself an artist. Mr. James showed me how to shade and make a drawing come alive. He said I had the talent of Rosa Bonheur, who was a well-known English artist. Boy, I tell you, that made me feel about ten feet tall!

"When I was nineteen I married a forest ranger. That lasted four years. Next I married a cowboy and we were together, lived and worked on ranches all over Nevada, for a long time but eventually we went our separate ways.

"Most all my life I've been on the desert, chasing cows and doing all those things you've gotta do on a ranch. That was the way of life I felt most comfortable with. But my shining star, the thing I always wanted but never had much time for, was to be a writer and an artist like Will James was."

Jewelle picks up a stack of paper and says, "This is my book, *Blazes of Black Rock Range*." She lays it aside. "I'm about finished writing. I'll illustrate it and then I'm going to hunt for a publisher. I'm not in a big hurry. See, I've been working at it for ten or fifteen years. I've got three tablets completely filled and the first was getting so dog-eared, faded and worn, I had to redo it.

"The story is about a bucking horse named Blazes. He is a reddish palomino, the color of fire, and he gets taken into a bucking string. He is a real man-hater but Ryn, he's the good guy, the hero, he ... well, better not tell you what happens or you won't wanna buy it when the book comes out. Let me just say it's a good story."

As Jewelle talks, the sun slides toward the horizon and the heat of the day begins to dissipate. Finally Jewelle takes her tablet inside to the kitchen table and by the light from a bare electric bulb she works on her manuscript, telling about a mustang that drops his head to drink from the water hole and the coyote serenading the night and the stars twinkling like fragments of shiny glass against the basalt-black of the sky.

ROSS PLUMMER

Ross Plummer leans on his walking cane, staring across the pasture where a mare and her colt graze.

He shades his eyes from the glare of the sun poised on the lip of the high, blue sky and comments, "Sure is pretty, ain't it? Makes me proud to be a Nevada native."

The sun drops behind the hill and the clouds catch fire and burn gold and red as Ross tells he was born at Mineral Hill, a mining boomtown in central Nevada, in 1891. "My father was one of the founders of Mineral Hill but by the time I remember, it had long since gone bust. There were old-timers around there, living in shacks, but things were pretty well dead.

"My father was born a miner, lived and breathed gold. He used to tell stories about going prospecting in the Black Hills of South Dakota, back when it was still Indian country. He came to California, walked all the way from San Francisco to Reno.

According to him they took seven million dollars' worth of silver out of Mineral Hill, but we never saw it. Hell, we had enough to get by and that's all that counts.

"Personally, I never cared much for mining. What I liked were horses, liked everything about them. There were nine of us in the family, seven boys and we all buckarooed. We used to run mustangs, set up a relay system and run small herds of wild horses in a circle 'til they got tired and we could drive them into a corral.

"Another way we gathered mustangs was to build a trap around a water hole on the desert. Made the corral from willow sticks wove together and a gate from a wood frame and gunnysacks forming a curtain.

"The way it worked was we dug a hole not far away where we could hide. A rope was strung from the gate to the hole. We would let the thirsty horses come into the corral — it would usually be at night — give a quick tug on the rope and the curtain would drop down blocking off the opening. When this happened the wild horses would race around looking for a way out but they never once tried to go through the gunnysack curtain. We caught hundreds of horses that way. The better ones we cut out and broke to ride because you got more for a saddle horse than a plug.

"Father had us boys ride herd over our brood mares in the spring when they were foaling. That was boring and so one of us would stay with the herd while the others rode off and tried to drive in bands of wild mustangs. Sometimes the wild horses would come in one side and out the other but other times they would mingle with the tame horses and we could drive them

into corrals and separate out the wild ones.

"Along about 1910 came a bad winter, a lot of snow came off fast and caused flooding. The railroad running between the mainline at Palisade and Eureka washed out. Two of my brothers and I went into business together operating a stage and carrying the mail. Made the run twice a week. Had two seats in the back of a wagon for passengers and I will tell you this, it was a mighty long and rugged trip. Took two full days. One night we stayed at the folks' ranch and then a night on either end in a hotel. Good weather we could use one team to pull the wagon but during bad weather we added another team. Ran the stage for four years.

"After that I went back to the ranch. Saw my father get killed there. We were busy stacking hay. Father rode up to turn water into the field we were finishing. I just happened to be watching as a whirlwind came up, picked up some loose hay out of a windrow and spooked Father's horse. It jumped sideways. Father was bucked off, landed wrong and it killed him. I carried him home. Those things happen on a ranch. You have to take them in stride.

"While I was running the ranch I became acquainted with the schoolteacher over to the JD ranch. Her name was Julia and we hit it off. All one winter I would ride 25 miles over to the JD ranch to visit her on the weekend. Come spring we got married.

"We had three daughters. When they were old enough for school we gave up the ranch and moved to town. By then I was 59 years old. I went to work on the railroad and stayed until I was seventy and then gave it up, walked away.

"In my life I've seen a lot of changes — from running a horse-drawn stage to watching television while men walked around on the moon.

"Lot of changes," he says wistfully. He takes one more look at the mare and colt and turns and heads toward home, using his cane for balance, making his way through the darkening shadows of evening.

THE BENGOA FAMILY

The Kings River country of northern Nevada is closed in by the Bilk Creek Mountains on one side and Disaster Peak on the other. Hereford and black baldy cows and calves are scattered across the broad sweep of the open valley floor where the path of the river is marked by a winding line of willows.

At the head of the valley, eighty miles down a dead-end, dirt road from Winnemucca, lies Kings River Ranch. It is an operation owned since 1941 by the three Bengoa brothers; Cleto, Chris and Frank. It is a ranch that remains firmly rooted in the rich traditions of the Old West.

Three families live under a common roof. The house, built of rock, remains warm in winter and cool in summer. There are few windows and though the interior is dark, it is homey. A long table, with chairs pulled tight to it, dominates the dining room. The kitchen is large. The women take turns preparing meals. Off the kitchen is a walk-in cooler stocked with four sides of beef and enough food to last a month.

The men work outside, tending to the business of operating the sprawling ranch. Because of its isolation they cannot run to town every time they need a part. They fix what needs fixing and take pride in their self-sufficiency.

The brothers make a few concessions to the modern world. They no longer keep work horses. In the barn, collars and harness hang from rafters and pegs on the wall. Work once done by horse power has been taken over by tractors and farm equipment. But they still use dogs to work the sheep and ride horseback to tend and move the cattle.

The Bengoas live and work together. They have little need for the fast-paced modern world and are content to live a secluded existence, together, as family.

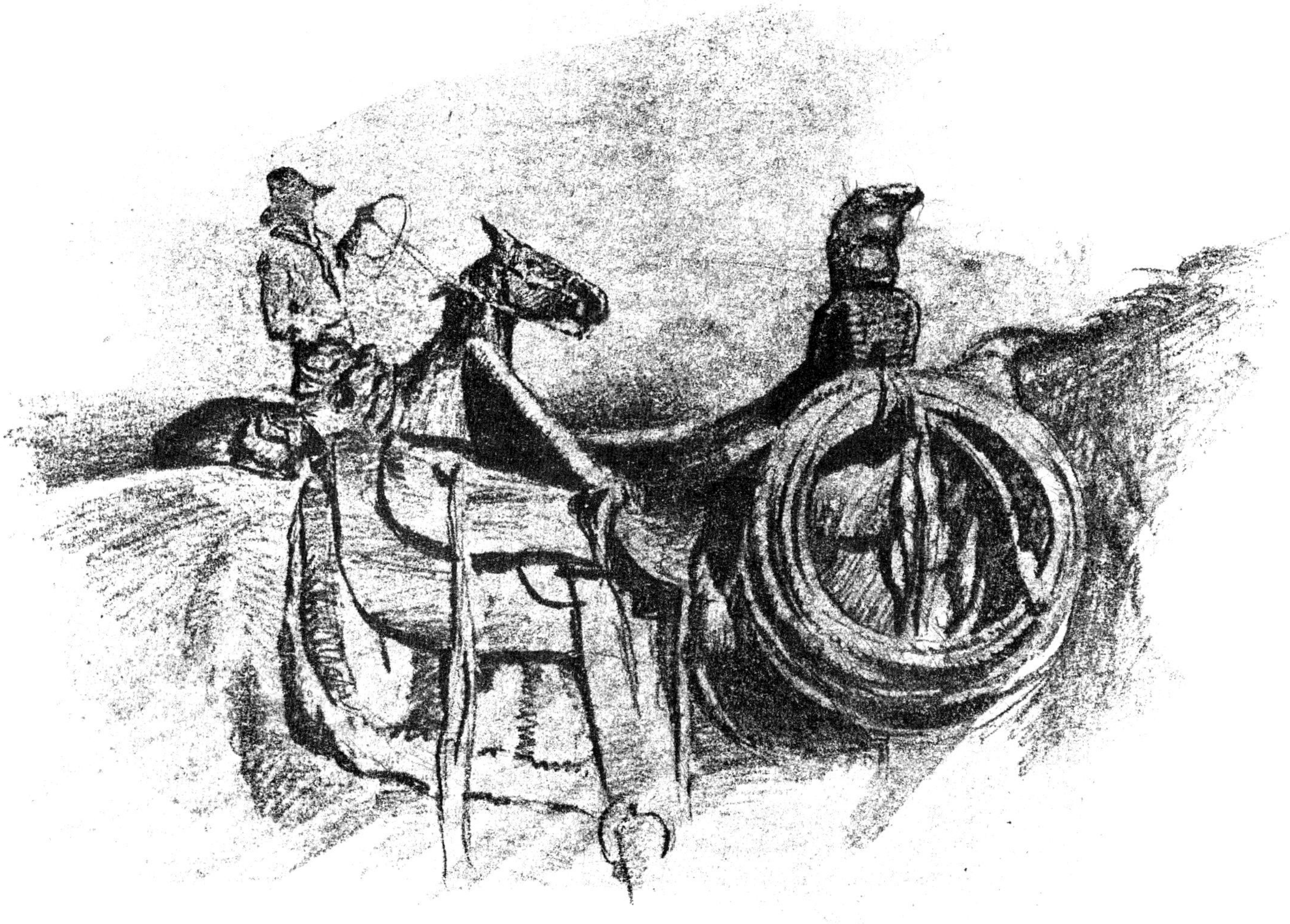

WESTERN JUNIPER

CHAPTER 4

Junipers love wide-open spaces. They spread out and give each other elbow room. Across the broad sweep of the West the small evergreens add polka dot color and life to the dry hills and flat plains.

Each juniper is one of a kind, formed by soil conditions and the availability of moisture within the reach of its deep root system. In old age — they can live as long as 3,000 years — their limbs become gnarled and ghost-like.

Junipers are scattered across the rangeland of Fort Schellbourne Ranch. Between the trees are the remnants of the changing West; fading trails, crumbling walls, abandoned wagons, ore buckets, barbed wire, rusting hulks of automobiles.... Each relic has its place in time, resting in piles and in layers like an unearthed archeological site.

Charlie Vaccaro has time on his hands. He talks about herding sheep and prospecting. His wife, lying in her bed in the front room, barely clings to life. Each breath is an effort. And Charlie, the man who loved to roam the hills following sheep and looking for minerals, is confined by his love for his wife.

Howard Miller spent his entire life on Crow Camp Ranch and he takes pride in two things; his cattle and the fact that he has done nothing that will leave a permanent scar on the land.

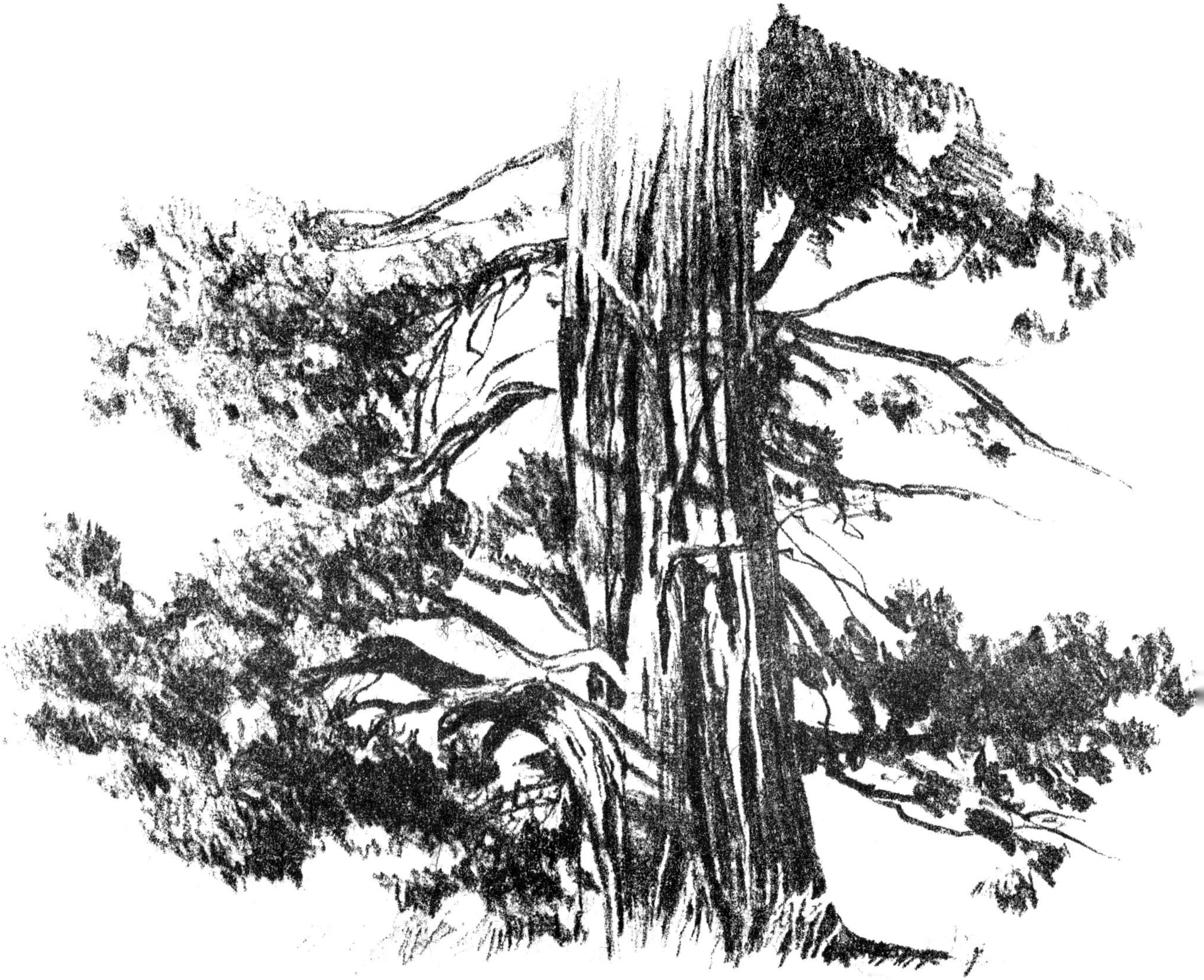

RUTH AND JUY RUSSELL

The history of Schellbourne lies scattered; abandoned buckboards, rusting hulks of automobiles, horseshoes, harness, chips of obsidian and bits of blued glass, enameled pans half-buried in the ground, wood stoves, a hay derrick, buildings collapsing in on themselves. Fragments of forgotten lives.

Juy and Ruth Russell have owned Schellbourne Ranch since 1947. Juy pushes up the bill of his baseball cap, peers over the top of his glasses and offers, "We know some of the history. Not all of it. Lot went on here.

"This used to be an Indian burial ground. I've come across old trade beads, arrowheads, spearpoints, that sort of thing. When the Pony Express came through this was one of their stations. The route ran clear from Sacramento, California to St. Joe, Missouri. Came out — see that gap there on the far side of the valley? — came out there. Went through here and right up the draw. That was in 1860 and '61. Eighteen months, that was all they ran 'er. A lot of people don't know that.

"Fellow came through a couple years back. Said he was from the St. Joe Pony Express Museum. According to him we've got the only express station still standing in Nevada.

"After the company went belly-up they made this into a stage stop. Guess this one time the stage was coming down through the draw there and an Indian, hiding up in that rimrock, took a pot shot, hit the driver in the neck and killed him. The horses came on in, stopped right about here where I'm standing and the passengers never even knew anything was wrong until they found the driver slumped over on the seat. Years later, after the stage was discontinued, they turned it into a hotel."

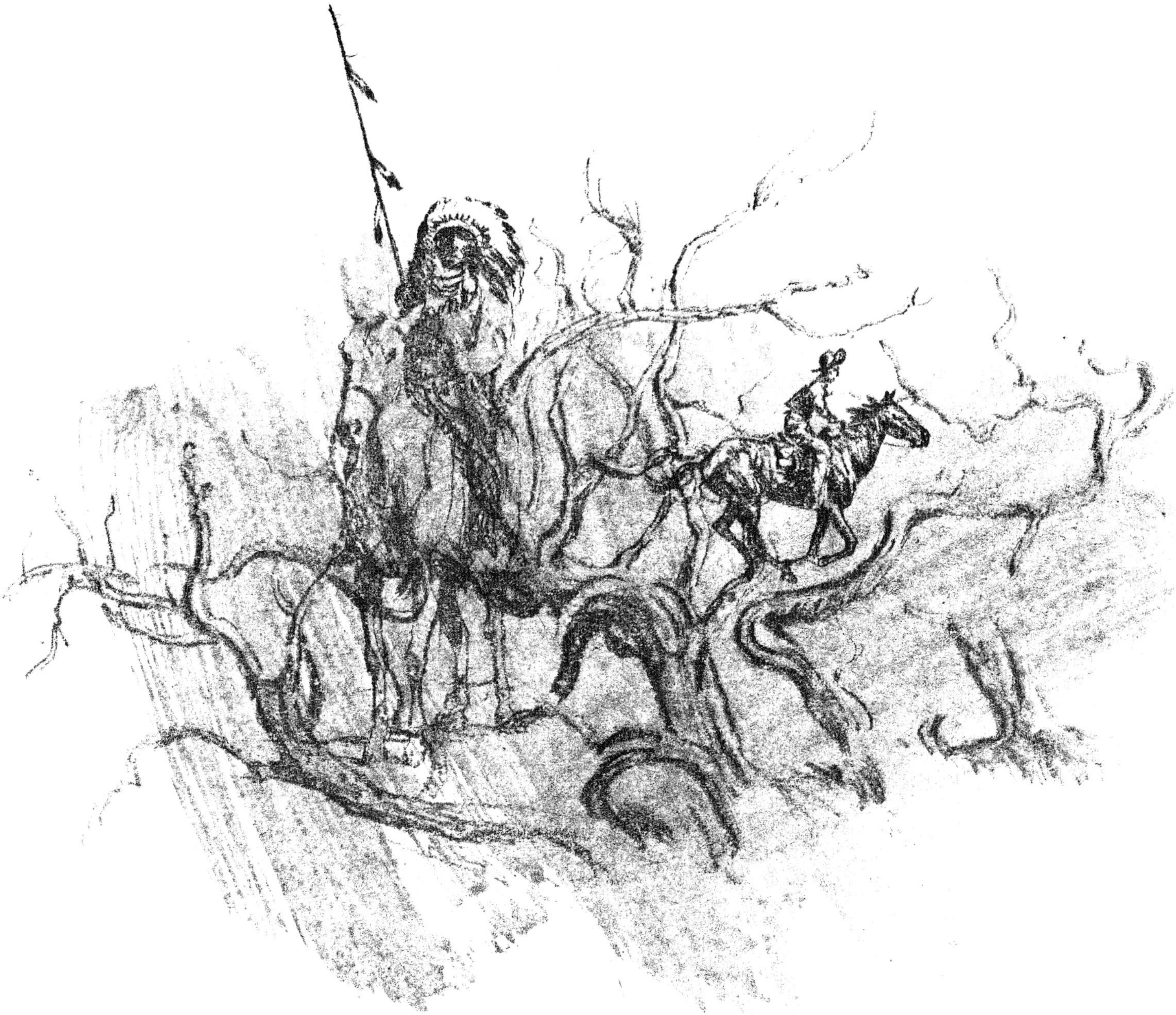

Juy walks a half dozen steps, using a cane, dragging his left leg. Ruth moves along with him, ready to help if he should falter. He pauses long enough to explain his slow progress. "Had a stroke. Crippled me up. Slows me but really doesn't bother me." He laughs at himself, goes another dozen steps, stops and points to a line of huge willow trees. "First men to hang in Nevada were strung up from one of these trees. Posse caught up to 'em here."

He moves on, stops, tells how gold and silver were discovered nearby and how miners rushed in and sunk shafts into the hillside. The town of Schell Creek, with a population of 800, was built here and a stamp mill established. Ore was brought from the mine on a tramway. All that remains are parts of a giant wheel and a cable with buckets still attached that snake up the hill toward the entrance of the old mine.

"By 1871 they picked her clean," says Juy. "When they hit paydirt across the valley they moved Schell Creek, lock, stock and barrel, and made the town of Cherry Creek.

"The old stage station was made out of adobe," adds Ruth. "They couldn't move it. That's where we live. Two of the rooms are separated by French doors. The one room used to be the post office. That's my kitchen."

Juy moves on, stops in front of an old building. "This is Fort Schellbourne. What's left of her."

The walls, made from rock quarried nearby, are caving in and the hand-forged iron doors and shutters are tipped at odd angles. Inside is one lone tree that died years ago.

"They built a fort here because there was considerable trouble with the Indians. When the town died the army pulled out. But the fort was used for years after.

"I heard a story once that old man Burke, the Burkes were among the first settlers in these parts, had to hide his family in the fort for three days and nights because the Indians were on the warpath.

"Whew. I'm all wore out. Ruth, give me a hand. I've got to sit in the shade for a spell. Right here. This is good. Help me down on this stump. Okay, easy, easy does it, good, thanks.

"Feels good to get off my feet. They don't work all that well. But I'm not kicking. At least I'm alive, which is more than I can say about a lot of my friends.

"Here's a story you might not have heard. I kind of fancy myself a storyteller. I like to hear a good story and I like to tell a good story.

"One day this Indian buck comes riding into town on a white gelding. Horse was limping on a hind leg, pretty crippled up, really favoring it. This buck goes all around town bragging how fast this horse of his can run. Of course, it wasn't long before some of the local boys tell him to put his money where his mouth is.

"The Indian goes to the town bank, tells the banker he wants to borrow a thousand dollars. Says he's got a sure thing.

"The banker wants to know, 'How many horses do you have, how many cows, how many sheep?'

"The Indian tells him a hundred head of horses, a hundred cows and fifty sheep. The banker agrees to give him the money but warns him if he loses the thousand dollars then he loses all his stock. The Indian agrees to it, takes the money and makes bets all over town, some at 20 to 1 in his favor. Like I said, his horse was all crippled up.

"Turns out the brave had wrapped wire around his horse's hind foot. He takes it off. I don't need to tell you which horse won.

"The Indian walks into the bank with a gunnysack full of

80

money. He gives the banker what he has coming, turns and starts to leave.

"The banker calls after him, 'Where are you going?'

"'To my tepee,' says the Indian.

"The banker tells him, 'Someone is liable to knock you in the head and steal your money. You should leave it right here in my bank. I'll pay you eight cents interest on the dollar. How about that?'

"The Indian just looks at him. Finally he asks, 'How many horses you got? How many cows?'

"Here's another. There was this guy had a dapple gray work horse and he was looking for another so he'd have a matched pair.

"One day he's in town and he sees this fellow leading a dapple gray and he calls to him, 'Your horse could be the brother of mine. How does he work?'

"The second fellow says, 'He's a puller. Hitch him to a tree and he'll pull 'til he drops. He's never quit on me.'

"'I've gotta have 'im. Name your price.'

"The second man drawls, 'I'm mighty proud of this horse but I'll let you have him for 500 bucks.' As he's drawing up a bill of sale he mentions, 'Grain him a little. Give him some good hay. He's been on straw all winter and he don't look too good.'

"The fellow leads his horse home, puts him into the pasture and it just stands there. He pops it on the rump and the horse runs smack dab into the fence. He takes a look at that horse's eyes and discovers it's stone blind. Hot! Oh my golly, was he ever hot. He hurried back to town, looked up the fellow who had sold him the horse and in no uncertain terms let him know

what he thought about a man who would sell someone a horse that was blind.

"The second fellow, he says, 'Now hold on a minute. Remember when I was making out the bill of sale? I told you that he had been on straw all winter and didn't look too good. Now isn't that what I said?'

"I could go on all day with stories like that. Need a hand up. Boy oh boy, I'm getting too old to even get around. I had that first stroke of mine in 1951. Ruth has done most of the work around the ranch since then. But you know, I killed a deer all by myself last year. This is kind of a funny story. A forked-horn got hung up in the fence by his hind legs, right alongside the road. I found him. Pulled a sixteen-inch monkey wrench out of the toolbox and I popped him in the head. I bled him out and then I had to have some help.

"Life's funny. You never know what you're in store for. Come on, I'll show you the cemetery."

Juy stands at the edge of the cemetery. Ruth walks around to the other side. She leans on a stick, watches Juy.

"There are nine markers," says Juy, "but probably a few more than that are planted here. Those three crosses over there were made out of wheel rims. Someone etched names in the metal but it was so long ago you can't read 'em any more."

A meadowlark twirls a lively melody. A calf bawls and a mother cow answers. Down along the creek the crows are cawing. Juy draws a long breath and lets it out slowly. He shakes his head, "Had to sell my last horse. For a long time I could still ride if someone would help me up on the stump and lead the horse over. But my legs quit working.

"I always said a man without a horse might just as well be six feet under. Yep, six feet under."

CHARLIE HALL

Charlie Hall pets the long ears of his hound and drawls, "All my life I've been a bachelor. Never could figure out how to support a woman. Done a lot of things; been a logger, rancher, trapper ... but the only thing I ever really cared about were my dogs. I live for hunting, that's fact.

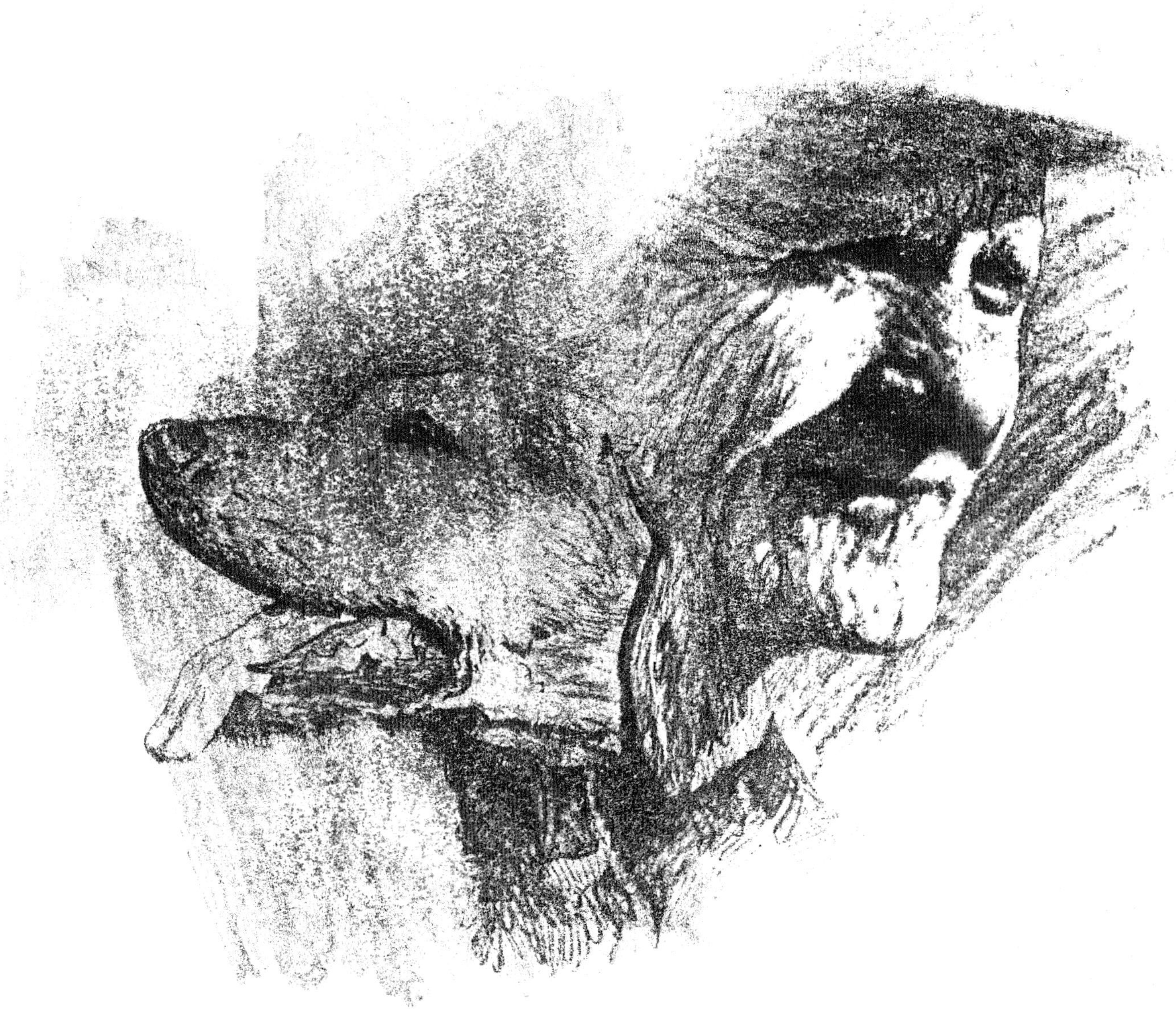

"Last few winters been terrible. No snow. No cats. At the altitude here in southern Idaho there's maybe one day in thirty you can run on bare ground. I think it has something to do with atmospheric conditions. If the conditions are right the scent will be there. Also, it depends on the dog.

"Had one dog, his name was Drum, he could run at two in the afternoon on a hot summer day. Never saw another with a nose like his. Old Drum was three years old before I got him. Had been a kid's dog. Lot of natural ability, always scouting on his own but he didn't know what to do. First time I showed him a track he thought I wanted to play. Once I taught him, boy, did he turn on! Had a lot of ambition, that dog.

"The first 14 starts I put him on he got cats every time. Once he got running he was hell on wheels. Had him for 17 years. Got so old I had to put him down. When you lose one like Drum it really breaks you up.

"Best dog I ever run was Jip. She was redbone and bluetick, white with tan patches. When she was five months old she treed a cat ahead of six other dogs. She'd take a track and move out, look over her shoulder a time or two just to make sure you were coming.

"Got my first really big cougar with Jip. We were up in the Sawtooth range, came across a big track and followed it twelve miles. Cold trail. But there were times Jip would lunge at the rope, wanting to go. Guess it was the way the sun would hit, sharpen up the track and she could smell it good. Never let a dog run a cold trail or they'll run off and leave you and I don't care what kind of a saddle horse you're riding.

"I could tell this was an old cat we were trailing, could see where he'd lie down and curl around a tree to sleep every few miles. Later on we came to a place where he had stood out on a high point overlooking the country. He must have spotted deer because he peeled off the point and snuck through the timber. From the tracks in the snow you could tell he had surprised a bunch of deer. But he came up empty-handed.

"It was getting along towards evening before we finally cut a fresh trail. I wanted to get the job done. A cat becomes a different animal at night. Night gives them security. They are as apt to stand their ground and fight as turn tail and run. Unless you're right there, they'll kill your dogs.

"Turned Jip loose, she made a circle and started singing. Had that cat run up a dry cedar just that fast.

"If you listen, a dog will tell you everything that's going on, all you have to do is know the language. A long drawn out bawl means the trail has cooled, sharp yips and barks mean the track is hot and the dog is moving out. They will sing when they get the cat treed. Prettier music you'll never hear.

"Down to this one dog now. His name is Trail. I've never been one to run a bunch of dogs. I'd much rather concentrate on a good one or maybe two at a time. Never more than two.

"Trail will probably be my last dog. I'm 81 years old. Can't walk the hills like I used to, have to hunt horseback now. I wouldn't mind being 90 and still tramping around in the hills. Trail and me, we're gonna hunt just as long as we can."

WILLIE WOODS

A white horse stands for a moment poised beside a hay derrick, then gallops away through the bunchgrass, juniper and sage.

"That's my horse Smokey. Must be all of thirty," says Willie Woods, seated at the kitchen table, staring out the window at the running horse and beyond to the snow-capped Ruby Mountains. "Don't get to ride as much as I'd like.

"Hard sitting indoors when you wanna be outdoors. Old age is hell. Now I know what Grandfather went through. He was Shoshone, lived the old way — hunting, fishing and gathering roots, berries and pine nuts. He got civilized, moved to town and there was nothing for him to do. He was lost.

"For as long as I remember my father worked on ranches and he drug us along with him. We lived in tents. Growing up that way all I ever wanted to be was a buckaroo. When I was 14 years old I quit school and went to work.

"Caught on with the TS outfit after the boss told me if I'd wrangle for a year he'd move me up to buckaroo. For 12 months I was the first one up every morning, gathering wood for the cook fire and bringing in the parada. At the end of the year I earned my bones, the boss gave me my own string and I became a buckaroo.

"I was there quite a while and then word came 'round that Russell Land and Cattle Company was a decent outfit to work for and they fed good, so I quit TS and caught on with Russell. It was a big outfit. Pure and simple, we worked cattle. There was eight and sometimes nine buckaroos and we each had a string of 15 horses, give or take.

"We ran on the open range, pushing the cattle 'round to the better grass. In the spring we'd be on the lowlands and as the weather warmed we'd move to the higher elevations near Tuscarora where we turned out. After that, for a month or six weeks you could either go on vacation or stay and wrangle for the hay crew. I'd stay, get up early, round up the mules and horses, tie them to the hitching rails. The hay crews harnessed their own teams but I always lent a hand on the tougher stock. At noon they changed to a fresh team. Those animals was never gentle. Every morning and every afternoon, after they started work, I'd ride in the hay fields and rope runaways. There was some God-awful runaways. Seen more than one man get killed. They was rough and rowdy days but they was fun.

"I never stayed on one ranch long enough to wear out my welcome. That way they was always ready to hire me back.

What set me apart from the common buckaroo was I liked to buck out horses, could never get enough of it.

"I was rough string rider. It was my job to break wild stock and if a horse got spoiled — anybody could spoil a horse 'cause we had buckaroos coming in from all over the country, Texas, New Mexico, Colorado, Kansas, Old Mexico and they all handled horses differently. Horse got spoiled, he went in the rough string and I'd work him.

"Fifty to seventy-five bucks a month was 'bout the going rate for rough string rider. You look at what people make now. If I had made that I'd have been rich. Kids nowadays always looking at their watches and saying its 11 minutes 'til lunch or 19 minutes 'til quitting time. Hell, I never even owned a watch. Couple of years ago I broke down and finally bought one, but I don't use it much.

"Used to be lots of wild cattle on the open range. They was crazy wild, holler and all you'd see was a streak of dust. Then they started feeding cottonseed cake and it tamed them down to where they was like pet dogs. Holler and they come running toward you. Cottonseed was no good, took all the wild out. Then about the 1930s they started dehorning. Instead of keeping their distance, dehorned cattle bunch up like sheep and you can't drive 'em nowhere.

"Another complaint I have are these fellars who trailer a horse to wherever they want to go, ride a couple hours, load up and drive back to town. And they call themselves buckaroos! We rode back and forth. Did it the way it was intended to be.

"First automobile I ever laid eyes on was in 'bout 1910. I was only eight years old. Dad was working on a ranch and the owner had a left-handed car to run parts to the field crew. When I saw it I had a devil of a time figuring out what it was. Didn't make sense to me how a wagon without a team could be traveling. I got acquainted with the driver and he'd take me along to open gates. It was fun but I really always felt it was better to ride a horse.

"Another thing, I never want to live in town. I'd rather be out in the sticks. One day in town is 'bout enough for me. I've seen plenty of guys get old, sell the ranch and move to town. Not a one of them is left. They just don't last. They end up in a damn saloon. No place else to go.

"I ain't ever gonna sell my ranch. They say a rough string rider never quits. Those that quit are dead and then, they say, you better bury 'im deep or he'll crawl out and try again. I believe that."

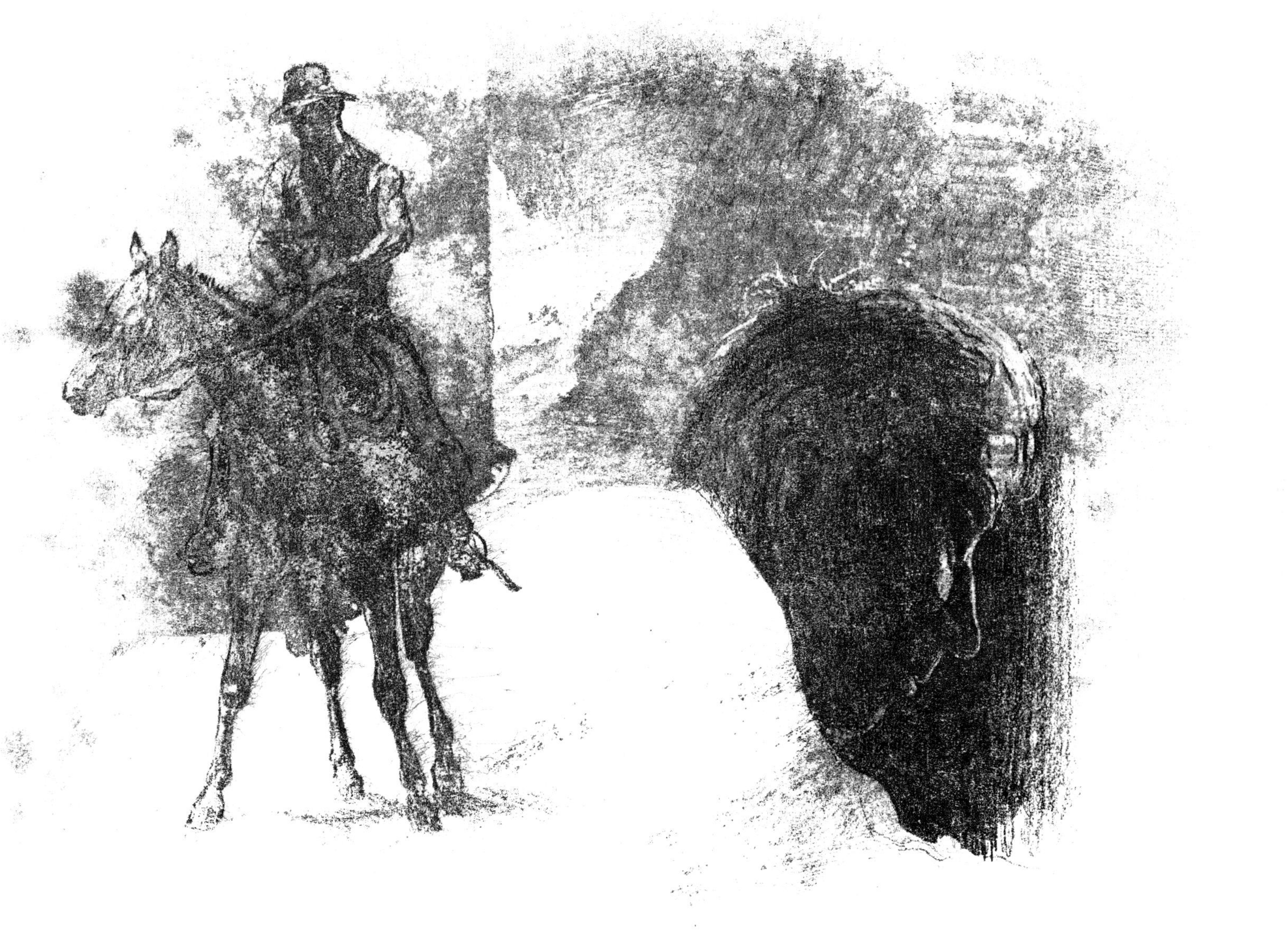

CHARLIE VACCARO

Charlie Vaccaro blows dust off his hard hat and with a familiar motion plops it on his head. He lets out a deep sigh and, resigned to the inevitability of it all, mutters, "This is all I got left. Lifetime of minin' ... this hard hat, few bucks in the bank. Sold all my equipment. Had good equipment."

Charlie hangs the hard hat back on the peg but before closing the garage door he pats the fender of a sleek maroon Mercedes sedan. "Oh, yeah, an' I got this hundred-year-car. Paid 65 thousand. Bought it for the wife three years ago, maybe been driven two or three dozen times. She can't drive, an' I'm gettin' too damn old to drive.

"Got me a Land Rover. More my style. I run uptown for groceries or mail, about it. Couldn't go nowhere even if I wanted. Have to stay with Esther. She had a stroke back in December of '87. Been laid up ever since. Better get back inside an' check on 'er."

His wife Esther lies in a bed in the front room of the house. She is sleeping. Charlie steps to the television, turns off the sound but leaves on the picture, for Esther, in case she awakens. He sits in his easy chair and talks in a low voice. "I was born in Prospect, Nevada back in '07. Nothin' there anymore. Town never was much, few houses scattered around the entrance to the Diamond Mine. Pretty good outfit, gold, silver and lead. Ran tunnels all through the hill but she petered out and they closed 'er up.

"Dad worked at the Diamond, then went on his own runnin' pack strings of mules. Had one operatin' over to Hamilton. In them days lots of miners were workin' their own claims an' Dad would pack ore to the wagon road. His other string brought wood, in four-foot lengths, out of the mountains. Some was sold here in Eureka for firewood and some went to run the furnace at the Diamond and Ruby Hill mines but most went to the coal burners. They were a bunch of tough fellows who cooked the wood down to make charcoal. A middleman bought the charcoal and sold it to the smelter. One time the middleman upped the price he charged the smelter, never cut the coal burners in on it an' that led to the Coal Burner's War. Five men died 'fore it got settled. They're buried up here in the city cemetery.

"Dad showed me all that stuff about packin' mules but I was more interested in minin'. Quit school in the eighth grade, thought I knew more than the teacher, an' went to work over to Hamilton on the leach plant. Was there through the summer and switched to Tonopah Mining. We were drilling, doing some development work and trying to find the continuation of the silver ore on Treasure Hill.

"After that I got into the sheep business. This is quite a story! We wintered on the flats west of Tonopah. Lived in a ten-by-ten wall tent. There was me, one other herder and the camp tender. Come along the first of March we split the winter band into two bands of 2,500 head each an' started north to the lambin' grounds in Antelope Valley.

"I would pack my tent, bed roll, coffee pot, groceries and the like on a burro. Stayed with the sheep. On the north side of the hills there would be snow drifts but the south would be open and the grass coming on. Great times they were. Air cool an' clear, fire goin', moon comin' up an' the sheep bunched on the hill for the night. Next morning when the sun came up they would drift down into the valley.

"We would go three or four miles a day. Never push 'em. Let 'em graze along at their own pace. Every five days the camp tender would come by to bring fresh baked bread and replenish the groceries. Always had meat. Kept a few wethers just for

that purpose. Butcher another whenever you ran low.

"When we reached Antelope Valley a crew of Mexicans would come in and do the shearing. They used the old-style scissor shears. The best could shear 120 head. Talk about a day's work — that was a day's work. A week or two after shearing, the lambs would start comin'. We would hire on a couple Bascos to help with the lambing.

"When the lambs could travel we took them up into the Antelope Mountains onto the forest reserve. As the snow came off we would start up and the higher we got the greener the grass would be. The forest ranger would come around checking, making sure we kept moving and didn't overgraze. Sometimes others working or hunting in the mountains would stop and visit. But mostly you would be on your own.

"Never did have much trouble with bears or cats. Once in a great while a bobcat would come in the night an' get ten or twelve lambs, kill 'em and suck the blood out of 'em, but most generally it was coyotes that caused the trouble. I packed a 30-30 and took care of every coyote I saw. Poisoned quite a few, too. The camp tender did that. Kill a wild mustang and make meat balls laced with strychnine, toss 'em around. Boy, got a lot of coyotes that way.

"Quite a life. Get into town once or twice a year, mainly just to have your teeth checked and take care of a few personal things. I was makin' a hundred bucks a month, had everything furnished, so was able to save the biggest share.

"After seven years of herding sheep I was anxious to get back into prospecting. Went out and picked up a zinc deposit on Lone Mountain. Had one of the nicest operations you ever seen. Took out the highest grade zinc carload ever shipped in America. Right out of that mine. Sold it to a big outfit, leased it back and there for eight or nine years pulled a lot of high grade ore. Made some real money. But I'm gettin' ahead of myself.

"Before I developed my zinc mine I worked in the Eureka Cash Store. By then I had gotten married. Worked with her family and since I knew all the sheepherders and camp tenders in the country, they brought all their business to me, a quarter of a million dollars a year. Then my wife up and died in childbirth. Blood clot. Her dying hit me hard. Didn't want no more of the grocery business. Had to get away. Tried sheep again, bought a thousand head of my own, but the going was tough. Hit some dry years and the lambs never gained like they should have, you were lucky to have sixty-pound lambs. Prices were down. You couldn't make no money at 25 cents a pound for wool and two dollars a head for lambs if you delivered 'em to Ogden. A lot of sheepmen went broke. I hung on for two years and sold the whole damn works.

"Well, I married another gal and went into the garage business. Never monkeyed with the mechanic part but did sell a few new cars, had Plymouth and DeSoto. Mainly spent my time developing my zinc mine and working for wages at Ruby Hill. Almost forgot, served as a Eureka county commissioner, was elected four terms. Lost my second wife due to a heart attack. Been with Esther now 25 years.

"I was telling her just the other day, 'Should have left you women alone and stayed with the sheep.' Those were the best days of my life. I was telling her that. Out there in the fresh air, nothing to worry about, nothing to bother you about, see the camp tender every five days. That was enough. Never was lonesome. Never bothered me at all. Best days of my life...."

Charlie goes to Esther, tucks the blanket around her shoulders. She sleeps.

AUSTIN PELTIER

May 1, 1925. The signs of spring were everywhere; grass showing green, apple trees in full bloom, calves on the ground. On that day Austin Peltier was home alone on the ranch, working a few head of horses in the corral.

Austin remembers, "We had a hot-blooded English stallion name of Desmond Day. Bred him to mustang mares an' sold the cross for cavalry remounts.

"Desmond Day was in the corral. He come past me and that was it. Always figured he kicked off to the side when he hit me, never saw it comin'.

"Somewhere in my mind, I've had dreams 'bout it, seein' Desmond Day comin' at me with his mouth open. He might have come back. All I know is I come to on all fours, could feel blood drippin' off my nose. Felt of my face. The right side was all cut up an' hangin' down. Couldn't see a damn thing. Got to my feet, staggered toward the house, got as far as the shop, was sick to my stomach, sat down a minute and finally managed to get inside to the telephone.

"We had a party line, rang the neighbor, several others picked up the phone to listen in, I said, 'Help, I've been hurt.' Then I walked to the kitchen and lay by the stove 'cause I didn't want to drip blood on the rug.

"That was where they found me, said I was in a pool of blood. Took me to the doctor. He sewed up what he could, put things back together but couldn't save my eyes. I ain't seen a speck of light since that day."

Austin digs in his shirt pocket, fumbles and drops a piece of jerky. "Never mind. The dogs or the cats'll get it."

He takes a second piece and rips off a bite with his teeth. As he chews he comments, "No flies this time a year. Good thing 'bout being blind is you can't tell the difference 'tween fly manure and pepper." He laughs.

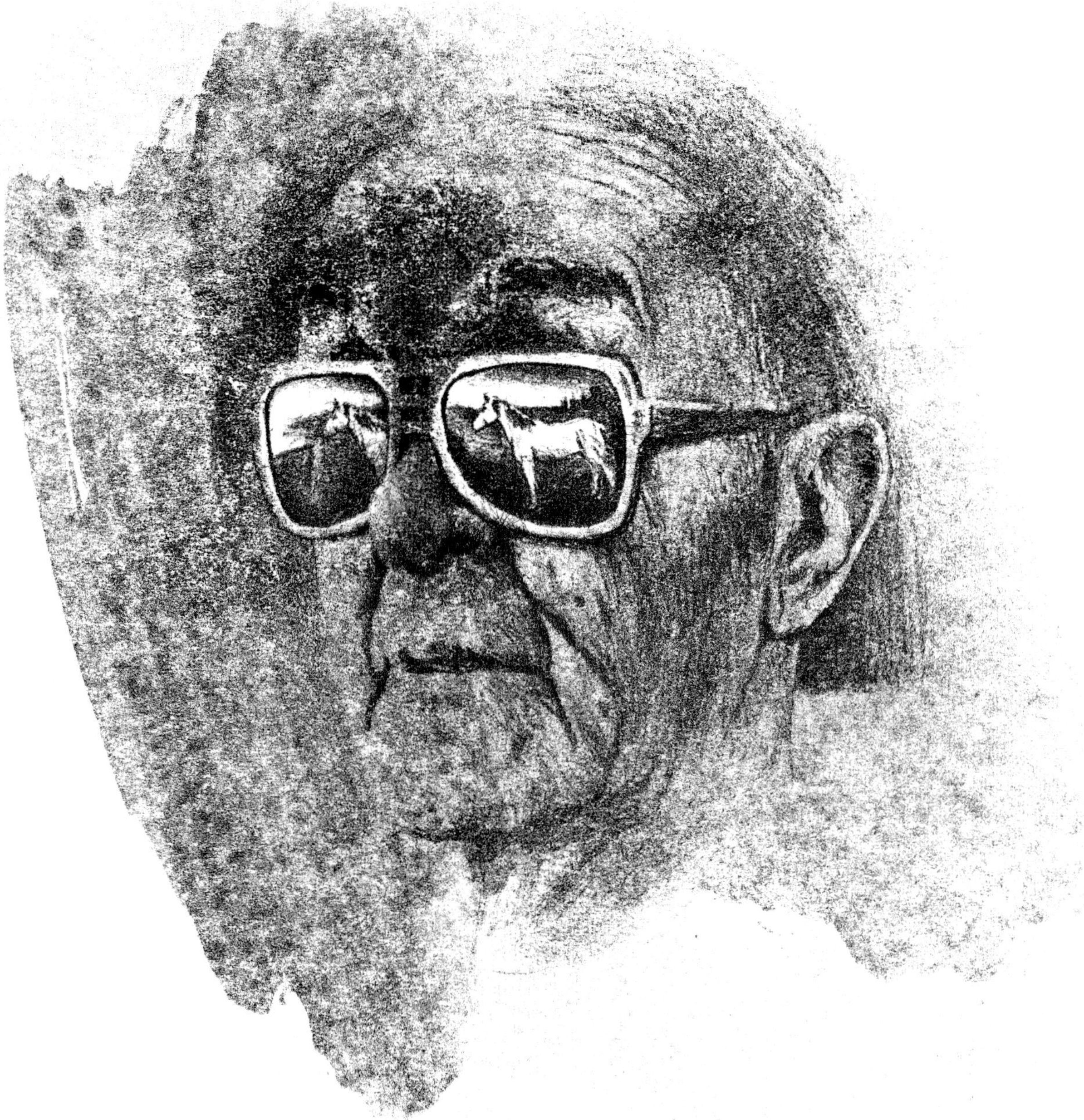

"In '27 they sent me to blind school — Oakland, California. They learned me to weave baskets, said that way I could make a livin' since I couldn't buckaroo no more.

"But I fooled 'em. Got a job with Elko County Telephone and Telegraph Company. Never laid eyes on the switchboard, went by feel. Took a couple hours to catch on. There were a hundred drops and folks'd call in and have me connect 'em. Say, 'Howdy, Austin, give me the ranch,' an' I'd recognize the voice and connect 'em.

"Had a lot of emergency calls; women havin' babies, car wrecks, one time even had a call of a robbery in progress.

"It was hardest havin' to tell someone that a loved one was no longer of this world. I remember the time I called Mrs. Friendly and I told her, 'Peggy, you better sit down. You sittin' down?' She says, 'Yes, I am.' So I tell her that her husband, who had been travelin' to Utah, had stopped to help a man change a tire and that someone had come 'long and that Ed was all right but the other man was killed. I hear a thud. I call, 'Peggy! Peggy, you there?' She fainted so I call the closest neighbor and have 'em go check on her.

"The telephone company went to direct dial in '52 or maybe it was '53. I stayed on a few years and then they didn't want me 'round no more. I come out to the ranch.

"I don't really give a damn 'bout bein' blind. Bothers the neighbors more than it bothers me. One time I was painting the house but every time the neighbors came by and saw me, they would make me come down off the ladder. But I showed them, finished painting at night, didn't make any difference to me.

"I tell people being blind isn't all bad — at least I don't have to run the lights at night. If I get lost I just keep goin' 'til I come up against somethin' I know. I go by sound, sun, direction of the wind, by smell. If I'm in town I can smell a saloon, barbershop, grocery store, hardware store. When you're blind you learn to use your other senses.

104

"The way I've got it figured is you come into this world with nothin', take the first breath and after that you're on your own. Some people've told me the public owes me a livin'. Hell, the public don't owe me a thing. I make my own livin'. Been married since 1923 an' supported her an' two kids, a boy and a girl. The girl I never seen. She come along after the accident. The boy, Robert, he runs the ranch.

"Few years ago Julia, my daughter, wanted me an' the wife to come live with her in Florida. Gave it a try. But I was like a hog on ice with his tail froze in. Florida's not for me. I like the pure, clean air of Clover Valley an' bein' on the ranch. This is my home. I gather the eggs, cook and clean house, make jerky. I keep busy. Otherwise I get as restless as a prostitute in church.

"Been over every square foot of this ranch and up in the Ruby Mountains, too." He points to the mountains. "Look 'bout up there. See that hole near the top? They call that Lizzie's Window. It's about six miles up there. Right at the top of a big basin. Just a hole clean through the mountain. I've been in it. Might be fifty feet wide and maybe a hundred feet high.

"This time of year I always tell people to look up in the draws an' see all the colors. Ain't that gold from the aspen an' the red from the poplar beautiful! Just love the way it looks against the green of the juniper. Can still see it all in my mind.

"Never held a thing 'gainst Desmond Day. After the accident I turned him out to pasture. He fathered many fine colts, yes he did. Ended up gettin' into a fence, cut up on wire, an' it killed him. An' that's that."

HOWARD MILLER

"Who happens to be on a ranch ain't that important. A man
can have a bad year, lose it all. But the land, it doesn't change,
it's here forever," says Howard Miller, standing on a rise
overlooking his Harney County, Oregon ranch. "I'm doin'
nothin' more than borrowin' this land. The object is to try and
leave it in at least as good of condition as you found it."

Howard kicks at the sandy ground with the toe of his cowboy boot, bends to pick up a flake of obsidian. He rolls it in the palm of his hand. "Indians camped here maybe a hundred years ago, maybe a thousand years ago. They used the land. They didn't own it.

"Freighters used to come 'cross here, travelin' 'tween Canyon City and Winnemucca. You can still see bits and pieces of the ol' trail, where the iron rims wore into the soil. They would spend the night there where the trail crosses Crow Creek. See that clump of willows? Right there.

"My father was a wagon freighter up in Northeast Oregon. The transcontinental railroad came through there in 1884, took away all the business, pushed him out. He went off in search of greener pastures, hit here, said, 'This is far enough,' filed on a homestead just north of Crow Creek. He returned to LaGrande, moved my mother and sister here. They lived in a tent until they could throw together a house.

"They had fifty head of cattle and at first the country was good. There had been several years of above-average rainfall, the bunchgrass was green an' tall. Other homesteaders came in but there was plenty of room for everyone to graze their stock on the open range.

"All the homesteaders built up their herds. Dad had 900 head but then the dry cycle came, the range withered up, got overgrazed and Dad sold off all but 200 head. He tightened his belt, hung on.

"At that time the place to the south of us, Crow Camp Ranch, was owned by Judge Joe Rector. He was a New Yorker. The first thing he did when he bought the property was to plant an apple orchard and rows of poplars to act as windbreaks. With the stream flowin' through the middle it was one of the prettiest spots 'round an' people from as far away as Burns used to come out picnickin'. There's still a few of the ol' apple trees left, not many.

"When Judge Rector died my brother Neil and I leased the ranch from the estate. 'Bout then the Depression hit with a vengeance an' ranchers were goin' out of business left an right. They'd just walk off, leave the land an' give what cattle they had to the banks. At the same time came the dry cycle again, we suffered the worst drought in modern history.

"Neil and I put together 400 head of cows and we moved 'em to wherever we could find feed. We'd use a hand auger, sink wells, sometimes go down 30 feet 'fore we hit water. When we did we'd set up windmills to pump it to the surface. There's always wind in this country.

"We were young and single. We slept in tents, kept moving

around. I'd hate to work like that today. We kept from goin' broke, barely, an' by '37 the economy was turnin' 'round, the market improvin', an' we were able to buy Crow Camp Ranch an' add it to the home place.

"I've put in seventy-odd years here. Never been anywhere else. Can look 'round at all the ol' horse-drawn equipment, remember when I parked that wagon, that hay rake, remember when people used to come here an' picnic and kids would swing in that swing. Wind swings it back and forth now. No more kids. This place is kinda like a museum of memories. Time marches on. I may've left a mark or two but the land, it hasn't really changed."

EPILOGUE

... we who pass do not own this land, we but use it, we hold it briefly in trust for those yet to come. We must not reap without seeding, we must not take from the earth without replacing.

The Lonesome Gods

Brock, Del * 1985 interview. Del died in 1988. Jason lives with his mother, Barbara, in Orofino, Idaho and attends Orofino Junior High School.

Collier, Cap * 1983 interview. Cap died in 1988. His ashes were scattered in Collier Park.

Dutcher, Ida * 1987 interview. Ida died in 1990.

Hall, Charlie * 1982 interview. Charlie died in 1982. His dog Trail died in 1988.

Island Ranch * 1978 interview. Henry Vogler III is operating Island Ranch. Henry Vogler IV is ranching near Ely, Nevada. Henry Vogler V attends White Pine County High School.

King, Frank * 1982 interview. Frank died in 1983.

Kings River Ranch * 1978 interview. Chris and Mary Bengoa and Frank and Ann Bengoa operate the ranch. Cleto died in 1979. Honorine remarried.

Lone Pine * 1986 interview with Clark Runyan. The pine tree is still alive.

Maley, Bridge * 1987 interview. Bridge is living near Lorane, Oregon.

McVay, Babe * 1987 interview. Babe is living in Eugene, Oregon.

Miller, Howard * 1976 interview. Howard died in 1986. Crow Camp Ranch was sold.

Morgan, Harold * 1989 interview. Harold is living in Eugene, Oregon.

Nuxoll, Clarence * 1975 interview. Clarence and his brother, Andrew, operate the family ranch near Greencreek, Idaho. The willow tree is still growing.

Parish, Ethyl * 1985 interview. Ethyl is living at Cassia Memorial Hospital Long Term Care Center in Burley, Idaho.

Parman, Jewelle Finley * 1985 interview. Jewelle is living in Eureka, Nevada.

Peltier, Austin * 1977 interview. Austin died in 1990.

Plummer, Ross * 1978 interview. Ross died in 1981.

Russell, Juy and Ruth * 1978 interview. Juy died in 1984. Ruth is living in Tooele, Utah.